TICKING TALKING COLLEGE ADMISSIONS

*How My Daughter
Got Into Her Top School*

PRAVEEN GADKARI

Print ISBN: 979-8-35093-862-3

eBook ISBN: 979-8-35093-863-0

TABLE OF CONTENTS

ACKNOWLEDGEMENTS:

THIS BOOK SUMMARIZES MY AND my daughter's personal experience, and what we learned was significant about the college admissions process from a vantage point of not knowing anything about it until it was late. Nevertheless, our determination to succeed paid off in the end.

The idea of helping other students like my daughter was the main drive for me. The book would not have been possible without the assistance of my two daughters, Aashika and Priyanka. They both were instrumental in providing content and editorial support throughout the writing of this book. I salute their commitment. The encouragement to write came from my wife, Anita. Without her support, this book would not have been a reality.

It is essential to point out that the writing style mirrors many different individuals and may sometimes seem incoherent, but that is because of the input received from many loved ones, inside and outside our family. I am a commoner like most people who desire to accomplish wonderful things. In this case, writing a book. It will show the reader that this work comes from someone other than a highly acclaimed and professionally trained writer. Still, I hope that readers give me the benefit of the doubt and do not shun this book for that aspect alone as opposed to the merit of the content.

In the spirit of full disclosure, I would not have successfully completed and published my manuscript without the occasional help and guidance from ChatGPT. However, ChatGPT has yet to author this book, as you will quickly discover while reading it. Anyway, I have purposely dedicated an entire chapter on how to benefit from the "Common Data Set" with the help of ChatGPT. The goal was to show how students and parents can leverage the potent power of GenAI in their college admissions research.

Thank you for giving me a chance, and I hope this book will help countless students and their parents in their college admissions journey. I also wish good luck to all my readers. Keep dreaming because dreams come true!

INTRODUCTION:

THIS BOOK IS A FATHER and daughter-story told through the complex lens of college admissions. Being a first-generation immigrant did not help in this journey. I had no idea of what this experience might entail until I realized that we had truly little time to catch up, let alone prepare a solid 4-year resume to get our daughter into a top-notch school because that somehow became her ambition at some point during high school. She was in the 10th grade when we spoke about this topic. It never crossed our mind that we should even be preparing for college in any way. I only recall someone telling me that there was a significant randomness factor in the admissions game, assuming you are within the range of the basic qualifications.

Long story short, what high schoolers and parents must go through if their goal is to get into an elite school. I know what is needed, having gone through this process quickly. Since we had less time, we had to work harder to get to where we wanted to be as the destination. Ultimately, our hard work paid off, but the overall process was exhausting.

The best value of education should be the goal. Most parents might share this view but remember that our children live in a different world. They have preconceived notions about where they want to go to school and where they want to live.

There has been an ongoing debate about choosing an elite school versus a best-value school. We always thought our kids would attend an Iowa school nearby. This Ivy League business only occurred to us during the pandemic. Moreover, when we discussed this topic with our friends, there were different points of view. Most readers will identify with this conflict and varied schools of thought regarding what is better. An elite college offers an influential alumni network, robust connections, and unparalleled opportunities. We can go on beating this issue to death. I tell parents and students that this is a personal decision that should be made by weighing all the viable options at the family's disposal. The financial aspect is one of the most crucial factors, but not the only one.

I cannot resist the temptation to mention another issue about college admissions, which may even be pertinent across the globe.

College admissions are considered an equity and access problem by many. There is a growing concern that the process needs to be more equitable and favor students from affluent backgrounds or those with access to specialized resources and support.

Factors including the increasing selectivity of colleges, the role of standardized tests in admissions decisions, and the pressure on students to build impressive resumes and extracurricular profiles play a significant role. Moreover, there is a recognition that historically marginalized sections, such as low-income students and students of color, face systemic challenges that make it difficult to gain admission to selective colleges.

As a result, there is a growing movement to reform the college admissions process to make it more inclusive. It includes initiatives to increase access to resources and support for underserved students, such as college counseling and test preparation programs. It also has efforts to rethink admissions criteria to focus more on students' potential and resilience than their academic and extracurricular achievements.

This issue is complex and multifaceted and will remain an important topic of discussion for years. Regardless of what people are talking about, our job as parents and students is to stay focused and within our shared objective of getting into a good college to pursue higher education.

This book will give you the necessary tools to be successful in your college application process. It will also inspire you to dream big.

"Success is not final, failure is not fatal: it is the courage to continue that counts."

- WINSTON CHURCHILL

CHAPTER 1:
Belief in oneself

WELCOME TO A WORLD WHERE you can be who you want to be. Thank you for choosing to read this book, and the fact that you have chosen to walk down this path is a sign of beautiful things waiting to happen in your life. What I said in the previous sentence applies to the parent as well as to the student. I call this journey a path to self-discovery and self-realization, wherein one will surely recognize one's true potential no matter how complex this process may seem.

How many of you have either read the Harry Potter books or watched the Harry Potter movies? What is it that makes Harry unique? Think about that for a second and imagine if you were Harry Potter. For those who may not enjoy the legend of Harry Potter, think about a superhero from one of the Marvel movies or the protagonist from The Hunger Games. What is it that makes whichever character you have picked mind-blowing? There must be something, right? I want you to believe that you are either Harry, Katniss Everdeen, or one of the superheroes, and your world is just like the world of one of these personalities.

Receiving his letter to attend Hogwarts School of Witchcraft and Wizardry and finding out he is a wizard was a life-changing moment for Harry Potter. [Rowling, J.K. Harry Potter and the Sorcerer's Stone. Scholastic, 1998]. It marked the beginning of his journey into the magical world, which he had previously not known. Harry had always felt out of place in his mundane life with the Dursleys, but finally, he found a place where he belonged. Hogwarts became Harry's home, and the friends he made there became his family. The letter opened a world of possibility for Harry, allowing him to embrace his magical abilities and embark on a thrilling adventure that would change his life and the fate of the wizarding world forever.

Comparing this to an admission letter from a top-tier college can also be a life-changing moment for a student. It marks the culmination of years of sweat, dedication, and academic prowess. Like Harry Potter's letter to Hogwarts, the admission letter represents an invitation to the world of opportunities, a chance to join a community of extraordinary people, and to pursue their interests with like-minded individuals. The admission letter is a validation of the student's hard work and a recognition of their potential. Think of this moment: just as Hogwarts became Harry's home, the college campus will become home for the next four years, providing a tremendous experience shaping your future.

Let us consider another memorable event from Harry Potter's life. [Rowling, J.K. Harry Potter and the Sorcerer's Stone. Scholastic, 1998]. Winning the first Quidditch match for Gryffindor and becoming the youngest Seeker in a century was a defining moment for Harry Potter. Quidditch was not just a sport for Harry; it was a passion that allowed him to forget his troubles and focus on something he loved. Being the youngest Seeker in a century was an incredible accomplishment, and it brought Harry a sense of pride and validation that he had never experienced before. Winning the first match for Gryffindor was an even more remarkable achievement, and it marked the beginning of a successful Quidditch career for Harry. More than that, it cemented his place in the Gryffindor community for his athletic prowess and bravery. Harry's success on the Quidditch pitch showed him that he could achieve remarkable things and gave him the confidence to face whatever challenges lay ahead.

Similarly, we can compare a student's successful project or presentation to Harry's first Quidditch match. Like Quidditch, the project or presentation is an opportunity to display the student's skills, abilities, and learning. Winning the contest is like receiving a good grade or positive feedback from a teacher, which validates the student's efforts and provides a sense of accomplishment. Just as Harry's victory brought him closer to his fellow Gryffindors, a successful project or presentation can help students connect with their peers and feel like they belong in their academic community. The experience can give you confidence in your abilities and inspire you to pursue future opportunities with enthusiasm and determination.

Isn't it amazing to experience the lives of these characters? We all have the power to be like them, and it's just that we do not think we do. We all can get what we want if we believe we can achieve anything. I know that all of us have heard this at least once in our lifetime, but listening to it is not enough; the time has come to dream that you are a superstar, contrary to the opinion others may have of you. When I say that you must dream, I mean it because once you desire a specific state of your future life, everything will start moving in that direction.

I want the readers of this book to be dreamers. Allow me to suggest a simple technique. Before going to bed, think of your least favorite subject and believe that you have mastered that subject. Now, imagine your teacher congratulating you on getting an A grade. On the other hand, I want the parent to dream with visual images of being ecstatic, knowing that the child has surpassed all hurdles to secure an A grade. I want you to repeat this exercise every night for at least two weeks, if not more. Bingo, see the results for yourself. This essential first step might sound ridiculous to many readers, but I want all of you to know I have had this experience.

Jose Silva mentioned this simple method in his book about mind control. Based on the book, Silva Mind Control is a self-development program combining meditation, visualization, and other techniques to help individuals achieve the impossible. Students can benefit from Silva Mind Control in many ways:

1. **STRESS REDUCTION:** High School can be stressful, with academic demands and social pressures, including personal challenges. Silva Mind Control can help manage stress and anxiety with the help of relaxation techniques.

2. **IMPROVED FOCUS:** Silva Mind Control exercises can help improve concentration, which can be helpful when studying for examinations.

3. **INCREASED CREATIVITY:** Visualizing techniques can help tap into creative potential and generate innovative ideas.

4. **ENHANCED MEMORY:** Silva Mind Control includes techniques to improve retention, which can be helpful for students who need to remember enormous amounts of information for examinations.

5. **GOAL SETTING:** Silva Mind Control emphasizes setting and achieving goals. Students can use the program to clarify

their goals, develop a plan of action, and stay motivated as they work towards their objectives.

Silva Mind Control can provide students with valuable tools and strategies to help them navigate the challenges of student life and achieve their full potential. Schools and colleges have used it to help students study less but learn more. [Silva, Jose and Philip Miele. The Silva Mind Control Method. Gallery Books, 1978].

My goal is to walk you through our book based on the journey my daughter and I have experienced in getting admission into her dream school for a specific program. When we started, we needed to learn about the college admissions process, and for unexplained reasons, we did not read any book on this topic. We relied heavily on the internet for our research and abilities to get things done.

Congratulations, you are on your way to your dream school.

SCRATCH PAPER

CHAPTER 2:

Getting Inspired

ONE OF THE CHIEF INGREDIENTS for success in getting into your dream school depends on how badly you need it, and it is a universal truth that is most underrated. Remind yourself repeatedly that you want to see yourself walking the lawns of the dream school in between classes. Again, conjure images of you as a student doing things in your dream school. Parents should also conjure images of several things they could manifest, for example, visual images of them accompanying their kids on the first day of school. It may seem weird initially, but this is a baby step in how you train your mind to achieve what you want. People may dismiss this simple exercise, but here is my alert: ignore the power of the human mind at your peril.

Imagine you are in a classroom, and your teacher asks you to count the number of red items in the room. You start pointing and counting all the red items you can potentially see. Your view covers 360 degrees, and then you have a number for the teacher. Excellent job! Think about this briefly: did you notice the greens or blues while counting the reds? Yes, or no? You didn't, right? You ignored the other items because you were not looking for them. The point is you will get what you look for. Hence, go after your dream school the way you went, looking for the red items within the four walls of the classroom.

Let me be more specific about what one should be doing as early as 8th or 9th grade but remember that it is never too late to do any of this. My daughter and I had just learned about this complex process when she was in 10th grade. I wish I had done my research as a parent while she was still in middle school. Anyway, we put in a lot of effort to make up for lost time, and thankfully, it worked out in the end.

Identifying ourselves with other high achievers is what one should focus on because nothing is impossible. I recommend looking at college acceptance reaction videos on the internet. These students have recorded themselves and their loved ones while checking their college admission results. It is an excellent way for you to feel a vicarious pleasure as if it were you who got accepted to a top-notch school. Imagine the adrenaline rush, the over-the-moon feeling. Witness the reactions of family members and feel their emotions. Doesn't it all sound fabulous? It should be because the goal is to experience bliss and be joyful, knowing that you have finally made it. If you can enjoy this feeling like an augmented reality session, we are where we want to be, as this will intensify the desire to take concrete actions towards the final prize.

Besides deriving vicarious experience from these videos, one must pay attention to the underlying messages in most of them. There are myriad instances of students pointing to glitches in their essays or applications. It is human nature to open after a triumph and reveal vulnerabilities, an opportunity to learn from the missteps of those students. In many ways, it will be a revelation to listen to these students who never thought they could receive acceptance letters from such fantastic schools.

Above all, college acceptance reaction videos inspire other students by giving them hope, motivation, and inspiration. Here are some ways in which these videos can be inspiring:

They provide a sense of possibility: Seeing someone else receive an acceptance letter can help students believe that they, too, have a chance of getting into their dream school. An event like this can be incredibly inspiring for students from underrepresented or marginalized backgrounds, who may see few examples of people like them succeeding in higher education.

They offer motivation: Watching someone's excitement and joy as they receive their acceptance letter can motivate other students who are still in the college application process. It can remind them why they are working so hard and give them the energy and motivation to keep pushing forward.

They highlight the power of hard work: College acceptance reaction videos can also demonstrate the power of hard work and dedication. Seeing someone else achieve their goal reminds students that success is possible with perseverance and effort.

They highlight the importance of support systems: Many college acceptance reaction videos feature family members, friends, and mentors cheering the student on. That can be a powerful reminder of the importance of solid support in achieving one's goals.

SCRATCH PAPER

CHAPTER 3:

Demonstrating Leadership

YOU MUST HAVE HEARD ON numerous occasions that colleges look for leadership experience, and they emphasize this as another way to differentiate you from the other student applicants. Let me start with something from Harry Potter and conclude with something from Hunger Games.

One of the best examples of leadership by Harry from the Harry Potter series is the Battle of Hogwarts. [Rowling, J.K. Harry Potter and the Deathly Hallows. Scholastic, 2007]. As the ultimate battle against Voldemort and his followers starts, Harry finds himself in a leadership position tasked with rallying his fellow students and teachers to fight against the dark forces. Harry rises to the occasion despite his youthful age and lack of leadership experience, demonstrating bold leadership qualities throughout the battle. Below are some examples of Harry's leadership during the Battle of Hogwarts:

LEADING BY EXAMPLE: Harry inspires others to follow his lead and do their part in the battle by fighting on the front lines and demonstrating determination and bravery.

TAKING RISKS: Harry shows that he is willing to put himself in danger to protect others and achieve their shared goals. He takes calculated risks during the battle, such as finding Helena Ravenclaw to destroy a Horcrux despite the battle already beginning around him.

SHOWING COMPASSION: Despite the violence and chaos of the battle, Harry shows compassion and empathy towards Draco Malfoy after Darco's friends try to kill him, Ron, and Hermione. He and his friends return to save Draco from a massive fire despite being enemies for a long time.

MAKING TOUGH DECISIONS: Harry makes decisions quickly and decisively, showing that he can think strategically and act under pressure. He faces several tough decisions during the battle, like sacrificing himself to Voldemort for the entire wizarding world.

BEING STRATEGIC: Harry recognizes the importance of being competent in dire situations: he is vastly outnumbered in the forest by Voldemort after he sacrifices himself. He tells Narcissa Malfoy that her son, Draco, is still alive after the fire, and in turn, she tells everyone that he is dead so he can execute his plan. Others follow suit, like Neville sneaking up on the snake to kill it.

Harry's leadership during the Battle of Hogwarts demonstrates his ability to rise and lead in difficult circumstances. He shows that leadership is not just about formal titles or positions but about the ability to inspire, encourage, and make tough decisions when it matters most. His leadership example is a powerful reminder that one can be a leader regardless of age or experience.

Given an opportunity, I would also emphasize leadership when evaluating applicants. It is truly inspiring to see students who have embraced leadership roles in their communities, schools, or extracurricular activities. By taking on these responsibilities, they demonstrate their capacity to inspire and motivate others while positively impacting them. Moreover, leadership experiences are a testament to the development of vital skills such as communication, problem-solving, and teamwork, which are fundamental for success in college and beyond. From my perspective, observing the growth and impact of these leadership experiences is genuinely remarkable.

When reviewing applications, colleges look for evidence of leadership in various contexts — serving as a sports team captain, leading a club or organization, volunteering in the community, or doing a leadership role in a part-time job or internship. They are also interested in hearing about students' challenges while in a leadership role and how they overcame them.

They also recognize that not every student has had the opportunity to take on formal leadership roles. They value students who have demonstrated leadership qualities in other ways, such as academic achievements, personal experiences, or creative pursuits. Colleges are looking for evidence of leadership and a commitment to positively impacting the world.

Below are some general guidance on where to find more examples of college admissions officers discussing leadership or other topics.

One way to find examples discussing leadership is to search for articles or interviews with admissions officers in college or education publications. These publications often feature interviews or profiles of admissions officers, in which they discuss their approach to evaluating applications and what they look for in prospective students.

Another way to find these examples is to attend college fairs or information sessions, where admissions officers may speak about their institution and what they look for in applicants. These events provide opportunities to ask questions and engage with admissions officers directly.

Finally, many colleges and universities have blogs or social media accounts where admissions officers share information and insights about the admissions process. These posts may provide examples of how admissions officers evaluate leadership experience and what they consider strong examples of leadership in the application process.

The point is to demonstrate something tangible from your background. Let us begin by asking yourself the what and the how within this context.

WHAT?

The question is, what have you done to demonstrate leadership during your high school journey? Display what you have done in any area, within or outside the classroom.

- Helping your teacher keep the classroom clean, tidy, and organized
- Starting a club at your school
- Starting a non-profit organization
- Starting a for-profit organization
- Organizing a charitable campaign
- Mentoring someone

- Holding executive positions in school or local clubs/organizations
- Holding notable positions in extracurricular activities, ex, first chair in band or orchestra
- Having decision-making positions in sports, ex, Captain of the soccer team

HOW?

The question is, how have you demonstrated leadership during your high school journey? Demonstrate the impact you have had by quantifying the impact you have had by being in that position of significance.

- Saved 50 hours of teacher's time in a school year
- Helped mentor 50 students
- Honored 200 healthcare workers during the pandemic
- Collected $5000 for a noble cause
- Dedicated 100 hours training other band members
- Dedicated 100 hours coaching a junior soccer team
- Dedicated 100 hours tutoring other students

College admissions officers are looking for things that show leadership potential based on what you have done throughout high school. It is essential to display that you have done something noteworthy and the fact that it has had a positive impact on your classroom, your school, or your community. It is critical to display progression within a particular activity. What I mean by that is the growth you have achieved by pursuing that activity. For example, you were a student council member in your first year, a secretary of the student council in your sophomore year, a vice president of the student council in your junior year, and a student council president in your senior year. This gradual promotion demonstrates constant learning and improved maturity as you progress.

In my daughter's case, she had started a baking business called iCake during the pandemic. She also spent many hours baking cupcakes and donating them to healthcare centers in our city, thereby honoring our healthcare heroes. She also used a website called Change.org to create a petition. I will share details of how she set it up to effect change in her community, just as one of the things she did to demonstrate leadership.

But before that, here is a little background. One of Aashika's passions has been baking ever since she was little. Confinement during the pandemic allowed her to delve into this hobby even more. It was an accidental start of a baking business, encouraged by family and friends. The point is to follow your passion and keep doing whatever you enjoy because it will lead to something meaningful on your resume. You may or may not see it coming, but it will be worth the effort in the end.

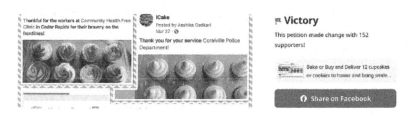

You can use change.org to bring about a change around you as a change agent, no matter how small it might seem. Their website on Change.org empowers people worldwide to initiate campaigns, mobilize supporters, and work with decision-makers to drive solutions. It teaches the best ways to gain support for your cause and make a change! They will take you through the step-by-step process from starting your petition to declaring victory.

- Create your petition
- Collect signatures
- Build momentum
- Reach out to the media.
- Engage your Decision Maker
- Declare petition victory!

They also provide steps to start a petition along with detailed tips to make your job easier:

- Select the scope of your petition: Local, National, or Global.
- What is the topic that best fits your petition? There is an extensive list that you can choose from.
- Write your petition title.
- Tell your story. Start from nothing or use Change.org's recommended structure. You can always edit your petition, even after publishing.
- Add an image (Optional). Petitions with an image get six times more signatures.
- Log in or sign up.
- Your petition is ready.
- Preview your petition.

- Create your petition.
- You can edit your petition at any time.
- Please share it with people you know or in online communities.
- Your petition will be visible on Change.org after it reaches five signatures.

You can use several websites to start a campaign for a cause you believe in. I suggest jumping into it and doing it. As per Investopedia, the 6 Best Crowdfunding Platforms of 2023:

- Best Overall: Indiegogo
- Best for Startups: SeedInvest Technology
- Best for Nonprofits: Mightycause
- Best for Investing: StartEngine
- Best for Individuals: GoFundMe
- Best for Creative Professionals: Patreon

As promised, let me conclude with the Hunger Games [Collins, Suzanne. The Hunger Games. Scholastic, 2008]. One good example of Katniss's leadership in the Hunger Games series is apparent in the first book/movie when she forms an exciting alliance with Rue, a young girl from District 11 who is also a competitor.

When Rue saves Katniss's life by helping her escape the other tributes that cornered her, the two form a strange alliance despite their differences in districts and backgrounds. Katniss takes on a protective role towards Rue, and the two work together to gather food and supplies in the deadly arena.

During this time, Katniss recognizes Rue's talents and empowers her to use them for their benefit. Rue learns how to set traps and uses her knowledge of plants to find food and medicine. Katniss demonstrates her ability to work with others, recognize their unique abilities, and empower them to succeed.

However, the killing of Rue brings the alliance to an end. In a powerful and emotional scene, Katniss mourns Rue's death and pays tribute by covering her body with flowers and singing a lullaby.

Through her alliance with Rue, Katniss demonstrates her ability to lead and inspire others, even during deadly circumstances. She recognizes the importance of working together, empowering others, and building relationships using their strengths to achieve success. The tragic end to their alliance underscores the risks and sacrifices and the importance of empathy and compassion in leadership at times of loss and grief.

SCRATCH PAPER

CHAPTER 4:

Volunteering

NOBODY CAN ARGUE ABOUT THE benefits of volunteering as a high schooler. In a nutshell, it creates a well-rounded personality ready to take on the world. Many articles on the internet will explain the benefits in detail. In summary, some of them are community service, networking, mentorship, skills development, career choices, and career interests. Besides the apparent benefits, volunteering lets high schoolers gain tremendous self-confidence. It leads to less fear of the unknown college experience.

This section will highlight the available resources to sign up for these opportunities. The first place one should look for this is at their high school. The high school usually posts such opportunities for their students, mostly regularly. I suggest they speak with their counselors about this if they cannot find anything on their bulletin boards. Besides counselors, they can also contact the other teachers and discuss this matter. I always tell students and parents to be open-minded about networking in general because you never know when you may run into someone or something special.

Large organizations like the American Red Cross and United Way offer various volunteer opportunities. Others like TeenLife and VolunteerMatch can help you find suitable opportunities around your choice, both geographic location and personal interest. Students may look at Big Brothers Big Sisters, Boys & Girls Club, and Best Buddies International for chances to volunteer in their local area. They could also investigate plenty of virtual volunteer opportunities in the post-pandemic world.

One of the tricks to search for something applicable to your area of interest is to create a LinkedIn profile for yourself and use that to find what you are looking for by going to other student profiles. Trust me; I recommend a golden tip that will immensely help during your high school journey as you start researching different topics pertinent to this process. I will go into more detail about the importance of having a LinkedIn profile later in this book. But here is the thing: if you do not have a LinkedIn profile, feel free to ask your parents to leverage their account for some of these things. This tool was a revelation for me and my daughter. It opened several doors for us, and I promise the same for you all.

Once you are on LinkedIn, you should be able to go to the search bar at the top to begin your search. Just type the name of any student you know through acquaintances who have made it to their top choice college. Once the search result comes back, the idea is to review their profile and educate yourself regarding the credentials this person has. Every profile on LinkedIn has several sections. Be sure to go through them and make notes. For example, a "People also viewed" section leads to other students with similar profiles. Then, there is another section on posts by this person that may give you an insight into their thoughts and about their endeavors. This information is usually on the front page, but if you drill deeper and click on the profile picture, you will see this individual's incredibly detailed resume. You will find About, Featured, Activity, Experience, Education, Licenses & certifications, Honors & Awards, Languages, Interests, and People also viewed sections. Every section provides an insight into what goes on to make a holistic profile. Look at as many profiles as possible whenever you find time throughout your high school journey. Once you start spending time doing this research using this tool, you will start getting better at zeroing in on things more applicable to you, your background, and your area of interest. Through this exercise, educate yourself on building a solid resume with a compelling story.

I have yet to discuss course selection anywhere, but the idea is to ensure that your electives align with your interest and passion for what you want to major in college. Other books talk about course selection in detail, but it should be a collaborative project with guidance from parents and teachers. You may need to be specific while doing this before entering high school. It is okay to have a general idea of your area of interest before selecting your elective courses during high school.

Let us take the example of a premedical student in college. You will notice on LinkedIn that such students have invariably volunteered in hospitals, free clinics, county health care centers, etc. The point is that these students focus on something related to the healthcare sector that is more meaningful to them. It demonstrates the student's alignment with their area of interest and passion. Again, investigating several LinkedIn profiles will provide excellent leads on feasible options for volunteering outside the usual organizations people typically think of. You may encounter something unique that may set you apart on your college application.

In my daughter's case, she demonstrated her commitment to volunteering by baking and distributing cupcakes to honor our pandemic heroes.

I read an article in 2021 by Emma Roth that listed "The 10 Best Websites to Find Volunteer Work and Opportunities". Here is that list for your reference.

1. VolunteerMatch
2. Engage
3. JustServe
4. United Way
5. Do Something
6. Habitat for Humanity
7. Give Pulse
8. AARP Create the Good
9. Feeding America
10. American Red Cross

I went on to ask ChatGPT (a tool discussed later in the book) to recommend platforms for high school students who are in the process of building a strong resume.

For high school students seeking to build a strong resume through volunteering, these websites are particularly suitable:

1. **DOSOMETHING.ORG:** Tailored for young people aged 13-25, this platform is ideal for high school students looking to engage in social change initiatives.

2. **UN VOLUNTEERS:** Offers online-only volunteering options, which can be convenient for students managing school schedules.

3. **VOLUNTEERMATCH:** With a wide range of opportunities, it allows students to find local volunteering roles that align with their interests and availability.

4. **CATCHAFIRE:** Great for students looking to utilize or develop specific skills, as it matches professionals and volunteers based on expertise.

5. **UNITEDWAY:** Offers a variety of initiatives and connects volunteers locally, enabling students to contribute to their community and gain diverse experiences.

These organizations offer a range of opportunities to help high school students gain valuable experience, develop skills, and contribute meaningfully to their communities, all of which are beneficial for building a solid resume.

I asked ChatGPT to suggest some more...

Certainly! Here are more suggestions tailored for high school students looking to enhance their resumes through volunteer work:

1. **ALL FOR GOOD:** With an extensive database of volunteer opportunities, this platform is ideal for students seeking volunteer work, including local and online options.

2. **HANDSON NETWORK:** This site can help students find local volunteering opportunities, allowing them to engage in community service and gain experience in various fields.

3. **HELP FROM HOME:** Perfect for students with limited time, this site offers 'micro-volunteering' opportunities, which can be a unique addition to a resume.

4. **WORKAWAY:** For students interested in cultural exchange and international experience, Workaway provides opportunities abroad to develop global awareness and interpersonal skills.

5. **HELPX:** Offers diverse work exchange opportunities, which can be an excellent way for students to gain practical experience and learn new skills in various settings.

Each platform provides unique opportunities to help high school students gain practical skills, contribute to meaningful causes, and build a resume that reflects a commitment to personal growth and community service.

Later in the book, I mentioned that as much as I love ChatGPT, it can sometimes be misleading unless you cross-check some of what it is saying. So, keep that in mind as you use this potent tool for your college admissions research.

SCRATCH PAPER

SCRATCH PAPER

CHAPTER 5:

Getting Financially Savvy

IN PRIOR CHAPTERS, WE HAVE referred to a dream school, assuming that the student and the parents have done their research evaluating different schools regarding competitiveness and merit-based financial aid, the two most important factors. Other metrics to consider are selectivity (the percentage of students who apply and get admitted) and yield (the percentage of admitted students who end up accepted). Most elite colleges try to zero in on students with early decision, which requires a student to agree to attend a college as early as December before most applications close.

In my daughter's case, she knew about the Ivy Leagues and the private schools. She was sure she did not want to apply with the early decision for fear of being locked out. She and I had to spend a lot of time on the Internet looking for a good business school. People might ask why you were looking for a business school and when your daughter wanted to study business. Kids are kids, and we all know that they keep changing their minds throughout middle and high school regarding what they want to become when they grow up. Yes, or no? The answer would be a yes. My daughter was no different in this regard.

Expect to start with a lengthy list of schools, but narrowing the list down is something to keep in mind as you progress through this process. A common idea is to narrow the list to three categories: Dream schools, Chance schools, and Safe schools. Having 2 or 3 schools in each category is a clever idea. Again, many of you may already know this classification, as it is a concept introduced previously. The various scholarships offered at these schools may be new to you.

People are rightfully curious about need-based and merit-based scholarships. There are many resources for searching for information about need-based and merit-based scholarships. Here are a few:

1. **COLLEGE WEBSITES:** You can usually find information about these scholarships on the college's website, including eligibility requirements and application instructions.

2. **SCHOLARSHIP SEARCH ENGINES:** Many scholarship search engines are available online to help you find both need- and merit-based scholarships. Search engines include Fastweb, Scholarships.com, and Cappex.

3. **FINANCIAL AID OFFICES:** You can contact the college's financial assistance office to learn more about scholarships. The financial assistance office can provide information about how to apply and any eligibility requirements.

4. **NON-PROFIT ORGANIZATIONS:** Several non-profit organizations offer need-based and merit-based scholarships. These organizations might have specific eligibility requirements, such as being a member of a specific demographic group or pursuing a particular field of study. You can search

these organizations online or through scholarship search engines.

5. **HIGH SCHOOL COUNSELORS:** Your school counselor can provide information about need-based and merit-based scholarships available in your area or state. They can also help you with the scholarship application process and guide you on making a strong candidate for these scholarships.

What I can say from personal experience is to try your best to look for these and leave the rest to destiny when it comes to the application process at the school of your choice. If you google, you will find many books on this topic that will provide excellent information. However, the key takeaway for us was that schools might surprise you in many ways, and one of them is when they give the impression that they offer tons of financial aid but only provide need-based assistance. Also, some schools work hard to attract talented students, and then there are schools where potential students must work hard to gain admission. This distinction is crucial as it will classify schools into two broad categories. There is no scientific way to differentiate schools in these two categories, but that does not mean this does not exist. Parents and students should closely watch this aspect during their research. One thing to remember is the constant debate about elite schools versus other schools, which is never-ending and often gets mired in controversies. Let me not cover this topic in detail as there is a wealth of information on the Internet for folks to consume.

In my case, I had addressed the financial aspect of this thing with my daughter somewhat early in the process. We discussed what these Ivy League/private schools offer and if there was anything special compared to the chances of getting in. The fact is that admission decisions are made in less than seven to eight minutes by an admissions officer.

We juxtaposed this information with other excellent quality colleges offering scholarships and reasonable costs, with admissions officers spending much more time reviewing applications. I had made it clear that she had choices, as deciding where to go to college is one of the most important things in a person's life.

In the end, it boiled down to multiple family brainstorming sessions. It should be a family decision. The family unit must address pertinent questions. How important is attending a particular school? Who is funding this education? Are there scholarships involved? What are your chances of securing scholarships? If an education loan is needed, will it be a student loan? Will it be a parent-backed loan?

This book will not waste pages delving into the history of admissions and how we came to this country's current state of admissions. I will leave that to the experts and the journalists. My goal is to work within the framework that has been established and not question it because it is what it is. I want to maximize our effort with our limited resources, acknowledging that this process is stressful for students and parents. My advice will help anyone applying to colleges to put their best foot forward. Students will be able to make a good impression on the admissions officer, at the very least. Again, this is more of a handbook to tell you how to do things in a way that will help your cause.

I want to address a few practical topics besides financial aid for college admissions. We will discuss some of these later in this book, although my focus will be more on strategies other books do not cover.

1. **Application requirements:** This includes submitting documents and the information in the application, such as transcripts, test scores, recommendation letters, and essays.

2. **Selectivity:** Consider how competitive the college or the university is in accepting students. Some schools have low

acceptance rates and are highly selective, while others have higher acceptance rates and are considered less demanding.

3. **Standardized tests:** Many schools require applicants to submit scores on standardized tests such as the SAT or the ACT.

4. **Extracurricular activities:** Most colleges consider extracurricular activities, such as volunteer work, athletics, or leadership roles, when making admissions decisions.

5. **Diversity and inclusion:** Many colleges strive to create a diverse student body and may have programs or initiatives to support underprivileged and underrepresented groups.

SCRATCH PAPER

CHAPTER 6:

Recommended Tools

LINKEDIN:

I HOPE PARENTS AND STUDENTS have heard about LinkedIn. Currently, having a LinkedIn profile is of utmost importance. Below is the Wikipedia definition:

LinkedIn (/lɪŋkt'ɪn/) is a business and employment-focused social media platform that works through websites and mobile applications. It launched on May 5, 2003. Microsoft now owns it. The platform is primarily used for professional networking and career development and allows job seekers to post their resumes and employers to post jobs. Since 2015, most of the company's revenue has come from selling access to information about its members to recruiters and sales professionals. Since December 2016, it has been a wholly-owned subsidiary of Microsoft. As of January 2023, LinkedIn has 900+ million registered members from over 200 countries and territories.

LinkedIn allows members (both workers and employers) to create profiles and connect in an online social network, which may represent real-world professional relationships. Members can invite anyone (whether an existing member or not) to become a connection. LinkedIn helps organize offline events, join groups, author articles, publish job postings, post photos and videos, and more.

Please do not think that people looking for jobs or people in a professional career are the only folks who maintain a LinkedIn profile. I will change that perspective and present an idea many of you may have just now thought about.

I recommend leveraging this tool in a potent way right from the time one becomes aware of one's desire to attend college. Creating a LinkedIn profile is beneficial in many ways. One of them is to document your progression through high school. My daughter and I used it to post significant milestones, awards, recognitions, and things we felt we might forget when completing a college application. It was an excellent way to centralize information whenever needed. Use LinkedIn in as many creative ways as possible besides documentation. Another valuable method is using LinkedIn to research other students and potential colleges. I will get into this in detail later in the book. Yet another avenue is to use it for connecting with students and admissions officers to demonstrate interest besides showing off your achievements. Let us dive a little deeper into these three areas of leverage.

1. **DOCUMENTATION:** You can use your profile as a database. Your LinkedIn profile is a handy repository for tracking important chronological events in your student life. Remember that you will need all this information to complete your college application.

2. **RESEARCH:** You can use it to navigate to other student profiles for valuable information. It will let you discover other activities other students have participated in. You can keep digging using keywords of interest to you. An excellent education and opportunities you may have never known will be available. Besides student profiles, this tool will help research colleges. Most colleges have a LinkedIn profile page and a ton of valuable information on diverse topics.

3. **NETWORKING:** You can send invitations to connect with admissions officers from the colleges you are most interested in, besides trying to reach out to existing college students. Connecting with alums and thought leaders can also prove beneficial.

Besides these core benefits, LinkedIn usage during college applications can help high school students explore potential majors and careers. By joining groups related to your areas of interest and participating in discussions, you can gain insights into different career paths and opportunities. You can also connect with professionals in fields you are interested in and ask for advice and guidance. It can help you determine which majors and careers fit your interests and goals and give you a better sense of what you want to study in college. Using LinkedIn to explore potential majors and careers, high school students can make more informed decisions about their future and set themselves up for success.

Now, delving deeper into the following LinkedIn features you will find helpful.

1. **ABOUT:** This allows users to summarize themselves, their interests, and their career goals. This section can help

others quickly understand their professional background and objectives and be a valuable tool for networking and building connections. My daughter had made this her introduction, a summary of who she is and what she stood for.

2. **FEATURED:** This allows users to highlight their most important and relevant work or achievements at the top of their profile, making it easy for others to realize their key strengths and accomplishments. Aashika posted articles (like the local TV channel, local business journal, her high school journal, the school district newsletter, and the local library website) where she was featured.

3. **EXPERIENCE:** This allows users to list their work experience, including job titles, companies, and job descriptions, to display their career progression and expertise in each field. My daughter had posted her jobs at Mathnasium and iCake.

4. **EDUCATION:** This allows users to list their educational background, including schools attended, degrees earned, and areas of study, to demonstrate their academic achievements and qualifications. My daughter mentioned her high school in this section.

5. **VOLUNTEERING:** This allows users to list their volunteer work and causes they support, demonstrating their commitment to charity within their communities and positively impacting the world. My daughter had mentioned her volunteer work relative to cupcake donations.

6. **SKILLS:** This allows users to list their areas of expertise and proficiency, making it easy for others to understand their strengths and identify potential areas for collaboration. My daughter had listed Networking, Sales and marketing, Business Insights, Business Development, and Business Management. It was all related to her area of interest, which was Business.

7. **COURSES:** This allows users to search for and take online courses and tutorials to develop new skills and advance their careers, all within the LinkedIn platform. My daughter had listed all her AP courses in this section.

8. **PROJECTS:** This allows users to highlight their past and current projects, highlighting their accomplishments and demonstrating their ability to execute complex tasks. My daughter had documented all the major projects she participated in throughout high school. She mentioned BOLD@ Olin, Change.org, Gateway Summer Program, and Young Women's Institute.

9. **HONORS & AWARDS:** This allows users to list any accolades, awards, or recognition they have received for their work, demonstrating their excellence and dedication to their craft. My daughter had mentioned Youth Salute 2021, Cupcake Contest for Teens, KCRG Student of the Month, Hills Bank Leadership Grant, ICCSD Student of the Month, BPA State Leadership Conference Award, Concours National De Francais, and National Honor Society.

10. **LANGUAGES:** This allows users to list the languages they speak and their proficiency level, which can be helpful for

international networking and collaboration. My daughter had listed English, Hindi, Bengali, French, and Korean.

11. **ORGANIZATIONS:** This allows users to list affiliated organizations, like professional associations or industry groups, demonstrating their commitment to their field and desire to stay connected with others in the industry. My daughter mentioned 1 Million Cups, The Technology Association of Iowa, and Business Professionals of America.

12. **INTERESTS (COMPANIES, GROUPS, SCHOOLS):** This allows users to follow companies, groups, and schools that interest them, staying current on the recent developments in their field and expanding their professional network. My daughter had followed all the colleges she was interested in studying.

LinkedIn can be a powerful tool for high school students applying for college. By creating a professional profile, networking with alums and college admissions officers, researching colleges, and exploring different majors and careers, you can gain valuable insights and make meaningful connections to help you achieve your goals. LinkedIn lets you showcase your skills and experiences, learn from others in the field, and be recent on the latest news and developments in your subject of interest. With a wide range of features developed to help people connect and advance their careers, LinkedIn is an indispensable resource for high school students preparing to enter the college and professional worlds. The best thing about this tool is using it effectively for "demonstrating interest" to colleges and admissions officers.

KANBAN:

Readers might wonder why I am suddenly changing course and mentioning this new tool for managing my workload. It is the right chapter and time to introduce Kanban to our readers.

Kanban originated in the 1940s at Toyota, inspired by supermarket stocking methods. It became vital to the Toyota Production System, evolving into Lean Manufacturing. In the 2000s, it was adapted to software development, and now, it is used globally in various industries for efficient work management and process improvement.

Here is how I see Kanban fitting into this picture. It is like a life raft in the stormy sea of high school workload and extracurriculars. Picture this: a simple board - a whiteboard or even a poster chart in your kid's room. You divide it into sections: "To Do," "Doing," and "Done." Each task and assignment gets its note stuck in the "To Do" section. It is like charting a course through uncharted waters. You know where you are starting and where you need to end up. Your activities and tasks should keep moving from one section to another based on how many you can handle. Tasks can only move into a section when another task moves out.

Interestingly, only a few tasks can move to the "Doing" section. It is about teaching focus. Think about it like this: you wouldn't overload a boat, would you? Same principle. Too many tasks at once, and the whole thing capsizes.

Now, this board needs to be a living thing, constantly changing. Tasks move from "To Do" to "Done," and new tasks get added. It is a real-time snapshot of where you are at. And like any good strategy, you must stop and reassess regularly. What's working? What is not? It is like when we were scrambling to assemble a college application strategy on the fly. A constant adjustment was vital.

And for those group projects? Imagine a shared board, a collaborative effort where everyone can see what is happening. When we had those roundtable discussions about college choices with friends and family, everyone's opinions and tasks were out in the open.

Most importantly, this needs to be a personal tool. Each student's board should be as unique as their college aspirations, just like how we realized that what worked for one family in the college search might not work for another. And just as we had to come to terms with our daughter aiming for an Ivy League school when we had always assumed she would stay close to home in Iowa, each student's Kanban board should reflect their unique journey through various activities and tasks, as stated before.

It is all about guiding our students through this high school and college prep maze. It is exhausting and confusing, but it is doable with the right tools, like Kanban, and the right mindset. Like navigating the college admissions process, it's about finding a balance, keeping your eye on the destination, and making those strategic moves that get you where you need to be.

Aashika was impressed when I discussed the Kanban board with her. She made me buy an appropriately sized board she could hang in her room and stickie notes she could use to write her tasks.

Here is a picture of a simple Kanban board with five tasks. Two tasks are complete; one is in progress, and two still need to start.

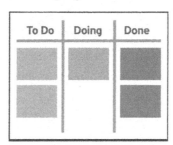

SCRATCH PAPER

SCRATCH PAPER

CHAPTER 7:

Standardized Testing

THERE HAS BEEN A VIGOROUS debate about this issue over the years. For a moment, let us not think about either fairness or equity and fuel this debate further.

My experience is mixed, even though I worked for the ACT for many years. In my daughter's case, she could have easily skipped taking the ACT because colleges were test-optional during the COVID-19 pandemic. I must emphasize that my daughter does not like standardized tests and obviously was not in favor of spending 4 hours taking the test with a mask. She took the ACT because she could demonstrate rigor and resilience in the face of an adversarial pandemic. I respect her for that.

Our philosophy was to do the best we could under adversity. As stated before, I am neutral when voicing my opinion about standardized testing. For me, it is just another tool to display rigor. It helped my daughter maintain a specific regimen and discipline in terms of her preparation for the test. She felt that it improved her time management skills as well. All these benefits were accrued because of her decision to take the ACT.

Again, should you decide to take either the SAT or the ACT, I suggest doing it with a sense of purpose. There is a lot of content out there that provides information and strategies for the test including practice tests. In our case, we relied on purchasing study guides from Barnes & Nobles. You can also find practice tests on the ACT and the SAT websites. No matter what you decide, keep in mind that colleges you plan to apply to are either test optional, test blind, or require you to submit the scores for one of these, ACT or SAT.

If you are looking for colleges that are test optional, where you are not required to submit your test scores, I recommend searching FairTest.org! Besides this website, every college documents their policy relative to standardized testing on their website. Like I said before, scores are just one aspect of testing. Now that my daughter is in college, she tells me that no student can escape some shape or some form of standardized testing even if it is short in duration. Case in point, every college course has a midterm and a final exam. The question is, do they seem or feel like standardized tests? My daughter's honest answer is a yes.

As you can see, there is no escaping the tyranny of testing (just kidding!) but seriously, try to learn from your experience every step of the way. Your experience may not all be good but, in the end, every experience is a life lesson. It will come in handy when you need it the most.

Finally, I will make a compelling case for taking the PSAT. As a high school student, taking the PSAT can be wise for several reasons. One of the most significant advantages of taking the PSAT is the scholarship potential it offers. By performing well on the PSAT, students can qualify for National Merit Scholarship Program recognition, which can lead to substantial financial awards during college.

Not only does winning a National Merit Scholarship provide financial support for college tuition, but it is also a prestigious honor that can enhance a student's resume and college applications. Colleges and universities often take notice of students who have earned National Merit recognition and may view them as high-achieving and academically talented individuals.

Additionally, taking the PSAT can provide students with valuable experience in taking standardized tests, which can help prepare them for other essential exams like the SAT and ACT. By taking the PSAT, students can gain insights into their own academic strengths and weaknesses, allowing them to focus their preparation efforts and improve their scores on future tests.

PSAT can be a wise investment for high school students, as it can lead to significant scholarship opportunities and provide valuable experience in taking standardized tests. By performing well on the PSAT, students can increase their chances of winning financial awards for college and demonstrate their academic talents and potential to college admissions officers.

I conclude this chapter by mentioning the vigorous debate surrounding standardized testing in America. The debate is happening because it has both supporters and detractors, each with their own set of arguments.

Supporters of standardized testing argue that it provides a fair and objective way to evaluate student performance and to compare schools and districts. Standardized tests also provide accountability for schools and teachers, as well as valuable data for policymakers to make informed decisions about education funding and policies.

Remember that GPA in one high school does not reflect the same GPA in another, and 40% of all American high school students graduated with an A average in 1998, whereas only half do today. That is why some people passionately believe that we need standardized testing. There is also this idea that test results are closely related to family income, but we know that it is debatable, and most likely not authentic. We also know that poor Asians, just as an example, score higher than the top quintiles of other ethnic groups. In many studies conducted by UC researchers, Standardized testing was responsible for helping discover minority students they would not have found otherwise.

On the other hand, detractors argue that standardized testing does not accurately reflect student learning and abilities. Critics of standardized testing say that it places too much emphasis on rote memorization and test-taking skills and may not capture the diversity of student experiences and abilities. Additionally, standardized testing may be biased against certain groups of students, such as those from lower-income backgrounds, students with disabilities, and non-native English speakers.

The conversation also touches on broader issues related to education, including curriculum design, teaching methods, and educational equity. Some argue that standardized testing can exacerbate existing inequalities and perpetuate the achievement gap, while others say it can help identify and address educational disparities.

The debate about standardized testing is complex and multifaceted, with no easy answers or solutions. However, it is a meaningful conversation as we work towards improving our education system and ensuring all students have access to high-quality education.

Regarding the role of standardized testing post-Covid, it is anybody's guess with colleges becoming either test-optional or test-blind.

One can argue about the impact of an SAT score or an ACT score in college admissions in this new era we live in, but what has changed is their influence in determining who gets in and why. The essays and the extracurricular activities will gain more importance in the future.

The real danger is not that computers will start to think like men but that men will start to think like computers. - Sydney J. Harris.

While this quote is not about standardized testing, it touches on using rigid, standardized systems to evaluate complex human experiences and abilities. Standardized tests can be valuable tools for gathering data and measuring performance, but we must be careful to rely on them sparingly or to let them dictate our thinking about education and learning. Instead, we must remember that students are complex individuals with unique experiences and abilities and that our education system should strive to recognize and support that diversity.

SCRATCH PAPER

CHAPTER 8:

Extracurricular Activities

IN THIS SIGNIFICANT SECTION, YOU display your demonstrated ability to commit to activities you enjoy outside the classroom. Extracurricular activities like volunteer work, part-time jobs, clubs, or sports are generally non-academic. The idea is often to pursue opportunities that align with your area of interest or the things you enjoy the most as early as 9th grade, if not sooner. The student should know that the extracurriculars they decide to pursue may directly affect the demonstrated interest aspect of the college application process.

In the case of Aashika, she was a little late in learning this perspective of the long-term impact her early choices would have on her college application. Luckily, she was able to gravitate towards a business-centric alignment eventually. I am glad it worked out for her, but that may be more of an exception than the norm. The point is to be mindful of your extracurricular activities and their future impact on your college application.

As mentioned before, colleges look for a connection between extracurricular activities and demonstrated interest. Again, the key is to show alignment between the two. Ensure that whatever you enjoy beyond the classroom is pursued to the best of your potential. You might think that I am contradicting myself with the statement I just made, and rightfully so, but here is the thing: you do not want to fake and pretend to like something you don't. I recommend staying loyal to your interests in the spirit of being genuine. Like life, this is also a balancing act between a burning interest and a fleeting, demonstrated interest.

Another critical aspect to remember is that colleges are trying to create a well-rounded student population on their campus and in the classroom. They want students who can make their class diverse and exciting with their backgrounds and interests. How can admissions officers determine if you are that individual who will ring in diversity? The determination is on the activities and how you have articulated them in the application.

Admissions offices often seek continued interest and commitment in a particular activity over a certain period. This pattern shows a sense of responsibility and leadership. For example, it bodes well if you have progressed from a member to a student council president in high school, meaning you joined the organization as a member but left the organization as a President. This progression will positively impact the reader's mind and will undoubtedly improve your chances. Try replicating this pattern as often and in as many activities as feasible.

When writing this section in the common application, I can confidently stress the idea of reviewing as many examples as possible from other students before attempting to document your own. My daughter and I kept reading as many activity lists as possible on the internet until we were confident writing our first draft. We both decided to follow the same process to compare notes and turn this into a fun, collaborative activity. It was unbelievable how closely our writing matched the ten extracurricular activities we had decided to document.

Here is the final list of the ten activities Aashika submitted in her common application based on the following character requirements.

- Fifty characters each for position/leadership description and organization name.

- One hundred fifty characters each for details, honors won, and accomplishments.

1. **Position/Leadership Description:** Founder/CEO/ Philanthropist

   - Organization Name: iCake (We provide financial support to the UI Dance Marathon Fund)

   - Description: Lead business functions of iCake that include managing sales, marketing, orders, cash, kitchen, inventory, vendors, and customer relationships.

2. **Position/Leadership Description:** Volunteer Baker/ Change Agent

   - Organization Name: iCake and Change.org, (https://www. change.org/HonorFrontlineWorkers)

   - Description: Ongoing cupcake giving. Brought smiles to 1800 frontline/healthcare heroes across 20 US States and 2 Continents within 2 months through my petition.

3. **Position/Leadership Description:** Freshman Representative, Member

   - Organization Name: Student Senate (Middle School and High School)

- Description: Brainstorm and implement ideas that enrich school ambience and promote positive social/environmental change. Collaborated with peers on many projects.

4. **Position/Leadership Description:** 3 Competitive Summer Programs

- Organization Name: Merit-based Kelley's Young Women's Institute, WashU's BOLD@Olin, Tippie's Gateway
- Description: Prepared and presented real-world business case projects. Connected with business/like-minded women. My team placed 3rd in one of the competitions.

5. **Position/Leadership Description:** Member

- Organization Name: Business Professionals of America (BPA)
- Description: Attend regular meetings, brainstorm business ideas, peer-to-peer review of business plans, attend conferences, and present business plans.

6. **Position/Leadership Description:** Member (Dance and Music/Vocal)

- Organization Name: Show Choir (2018 – Current), Choir (Since Elementary School)
- Description: Mastered new dance styles, instructed underclassmen in choreography, acquired techniques for stronger vocals, expressed emotion through movement.

7. **Position/Leadership Description:** Prior Member, Currently Assistant Stage Manager

- Organization Name: Theatre West

- Description: Co-managed entire productions that included leading stage design/build/setup and prop management, on and off stage.

8. **Position/Leadership Description:** Leader Board Member, Member

- Organization Name: Mentors in Violence Prevention (MVP)

- Description: Led freshmen in societal issue group conversations besides mentoring them one-on-one in acquiring a violence prevention mindset.

9. **Position/Leadership Description:** Indian Classical Dancer in Kathak (Since 2007)

- Organization Name: Friends of India, Hindu Temple Association of Eastern Iowa, Noopur Dance Troupe

- Description: Pursuing my passion for dance from an early age with numerous stage performances, including fundraisers.

10. **Position/Leadership Description:** Leader of South Asian Group, SA Representative

- Organization Name: Walk it Out (Cultural Fashion Show)

- Description: Leader of the South Asian group, met new people from diverse backgrounds, explored different cultures through various artistic performances.

Let me (either as the parent or as the English teacher) play the role of an admissions officer and review Aashika's first activity (As a Founder/CEO/Philanthropist). Here is my feedback:

STRENGTHS OF THE STUDENT:

Leadership and Initiative: The student demonstrates exceptional initiative and leadership skills by founding and managing iCake. Starting a business requires high dedication, creativity, and problem-solving, which are valuable qualities in a potential student.

Entrepreneurial Spirit: The role of Founder/CEO indicates a robust entrepreneurial spirit. This student has conceptualized an idea and implemented it successfully, highlighting their ability to turn vision into reality.

Business Acumen: Managing various aspects of a business, such as sales, marketing, orders, cash flow, kitchen operations, inventory, vendor relations, and customer service, displays a comprehensive understanding of business operations. This experience suggests a well-rounded skill set in business management.

Philanthropy and Community Service: The student's involvement in charity, specifically providing financial support to the UI Dance Marathon Fund, is commendable. It reflects a sense of social responsibility and a commitment to helping the community.

AREAS FOR FURTHER IMPROVEMENT:

Impact Measurement: While the student has outlined their role, more detail about the impact of their work would be beneficial. For instance, information on how much they raised for the UI Dance Marathon Fund or how the business has grown under their leadership would provide more context on their achievements.

Challenges Overcome: Mentioning specific challenges faced while running the business and how to overcome them would demonstrate resilience and adaptability.

Team Dynamics: Information about whether they worked within a team, how they managed or collaborated with others, and any leadership challenges faced would offer more profound insights into their interpersonal skills.

Future Aspirations: If the student could connect this experience with their future goals or how it has shaped their academic interests, it would provide a clearer picture of how their past experiences align with their future.

Here is the opportunity to leverage the summarized version of this extracurricular activity and expand it into something bigger. What I mean is that this student has an excellent opportunity to include the points mentioned in the "areas for further improvement" in either the "personal statement" or the "supplemental essays."

The takeaway is that the admissions officer will look for an expanded version of this activity because this brief content should spark their interest and imagination. The outcome is precisely what Aashika and I had in mind when we wrote this activity as an extracurricular activity. Take this concept further and apply this strategy to other activities mentioned in this section so that the student can provide additional details in their essays. This approach becomes fodder for more content in the college application.

Lastly, I want to highlight one more point about activity number 6 (six) on the list. Aashika realized that she must somehow accommodate all her activities in a limited list of 10 (ten) activities. It prompted her to combine two separate activities into one, the arts. You can see how she combines "Show Choir" and "Choir" under the same category. Combining similar activities is needed when there are more than ten activities to list in this section.

SCRATCH PAPER

CHAPTER 9:

Personal Statement

THE MOST CRUCIAL SECTION OF the college application process is this essay. The reason is that this gives the student a platform to express who they are, what they stand for, and which events have shaped their personality. The student should be using this essay to tell their unique story.

Remember that you can write about anything you want under the sun in this personal statement, usually between 500 and 650 words. Some books go into extreme detail and give you a blueprint of how to write a personal statement successfully. In our case, Aashika and I read extensively on this topic. We voraciously read whatever we could find, including what other students wrote. Through this process, we could see the intent behind documenting such a personal statement from the colleges' point of view.

Besides extensive reading and researching, I asked Aashika to make notes on exciting pointers she discovered during the investigative process. She later confessed that the notes proved invaluable during the actual writing. However, she also felt that a more organic writing strategy was much better than a more scientific approach. On the contrary, for Aashika, it was about pouring pure emotions on paper. Her recommendation is to let the words flow from the heart. I was amazed when I noticed that she had described an intimate and very confidential life event in her statement. Upon further pondering, I thought this was the epitome of a powerful personal story.

Expect several drafts and countless revisions to get to a final version you can share with someone you think should review your work and provide feedback. In Aashika's case, she sought feedback from her English teacher and me. At some point, we should strive to make it the best that we can, given the resources we have at our disposal. Luckily for Aashika, I was willing to walk the extra mile to invest in her essay both in kind, as one of the reviewers, and in money, as one of the financiers. Once we decided to take our version of the personal statement to an outside expert, I started looking for one. I took this task because I had the time and knew how much I wanted to spend, which was at most $500. I found a company willing to help and get the job done. They assigned someone who had worked with students wanting to attend USC, as this was Aashika's first choice. We were happy with the result.

Going back to the topics one should write about. As I said, you can write about anything you strongly feel, whether it is a life-changing event, an extracurricular activity, or a simple task like baking. I recall reading extraordinary essays about topics that I never thought were possible. The point is, take a leap of faith, take a chance, and I guarantee rewards if you are true to yourself in the emotions you feel and want to express through your statement. If you are confused, write down a list of potential topics you think you could write about. Keep revising this list over a period until you are confident that you have included everything there is in your life story. Once the list is ready, the challenging work starts with narrowing it down to two or three that look realistic or promising from a writing perspective. You can also combine some that may provide a good flow and completeness to your essay.

Another approach is asking yourself many questions that form the basis of your personal statement. I always believe that asking the right questions is more important than the correct answers. Holding on to this thought, let us conduct a small experiment. I will hire ChatGPT as an expert and here is what I will ask... **As an expert essay writer, which questions would you ask yourself to determine a topic that might be compelling to your life?**

START OF ANSWER.

As an expert essay writer looking to determine a compelling and personal topic for an essay about my life, I would consider the following questions:

1. What Are My Passionate Interests?
   - What are the subjects or activities I am genuinely passionate about?
   - What hobbies, interests, or causes have shaped my life or worldview?

2. What Are My Personal Challenges and Triumphs?
   - What significant challenges have I faced in my life?
   - How have I overcome these challenges, and what lessons have I learned from them?

3. What Are My Values and Beliefs?
   - What are the core values and beliefs that guide my decisions and actions?

- How have these values evolved or been influenced by my life experiences?

4. **What Are My Unique Experiences?**

- What unique experiences, travels, or encounters have left a lasting impact on me?
- How have these experiences shaped my perspective on life?

5. **What Are My Goals and Aspirations?**

- What are my short-term and long-term goals in life?
- How do my aspirations connect with my past experiences and present identity?

6. **What Are My Personal Growth and Development Stories?**

- How have I evolved as a person over time?
- What specific moments or experiences have marked significant personal growth?

7. **What Are My Relationships and Connections?**

- How have my relationships with family, friends, mentors, or others influenced my life?
- Are there specific stories or insights related to these relationships?

8. **What Are My Unique Insights and Perspectives?**

- Do I have a unique perspective or insight on a particular topic or issue?
- How can I share this perspective to engage and inspire others?

9. **What Would I Like to Share or Teach Others?**

- Is there a valuable lesson, piece of advice, or knowledge I would like to impart through my essay?
- How can my experiences benefit or resonate with others?

10. What Would Be Emotionally Resonant?

- What topics or experiences evoke strong emotions within me?
- How can I use these emotions to connect with readers on a personal level?

By exploring these questions and reflecting on my own life experiences, interests, and values, I can identify a compelling and meaningful topic that not only resonates with me but also has the potential to engage and resonate with my readers.

END OF ANSWER.

You can see how one can leverage the power of this tool to accomplish your goals if you need help or want a start on any topic.

Here is the essay Aashika wrote as her personal statement for the common application:

NOTE: Aashika mentioned situations in this essay she did not want me to publish. I will certainly abide by her desire, but I admire her narrating the problematic situations of her life in her statement, making it deeply personal for the reader.

START.

I was huddled in my room wrapped in many layers of a blanket as if desperately longing for comfort from inanimate objects. At ten years old, my brain wasn't prepared for the despondent conversation I had overheard between my nervous parents. They were discussing the end of my father's nonprofit, iTforTeens, which he had operated for almost two years. His firm belief in community giving had led to the idea of imparting technology training to the underrepresented and the underprivileged students in our area. My parents floated the possibility of leaving the United States—the only country I had ever known—and returning to India. The mere thought left me paralyzed.

My mother and I were separated for a few years due to her taking a job across the country so our family could remain in the United States, and my body was undergoing changes I didn't want to undergo without the comfort of her arms. As I fell victim to my xxxxx xxxxxx and experienced my xxxxx xxxxx, it felt as if I was isolated. I found myself wandering to places in my home my mother liked to spend most of her time: the vibrant sunroom, the cluttered office, and the once pristine, now frowzy kitchen. As sweet foods had always brought my mother and me happiness, I decided to start baking little treats to pass the time and feel closer to her. Little treats turned into cakes and cupcakes, and I discovered a strong love for baking, which gave me refuge from the challenges I was experiencing.

As my love for baking grew stronger, an interesting idea crept into my mind. I considered the possibility of starting a business. As I considered this path, COVID-19 hit. While it was a difficult obstacle, it also presented an opportunity. I started a baking business, iCake, which was founded on the philosophy of satisfying taste buds and bringing smiles to those who risk their lives on the front lines fighting COVID-19. I began my business with the idea that for every cupcake I sold, I would donate one to frontline workers. Making one dozen a week soon intensified to hundreds of cupcakes made and donated. Realizing that this was unsustainable for one person, I created a change. org petition that encouraged others to donate a dozen or more cupcakes in their neighborhoods and home countries. This petition helped over a thousand frontline workers around the world, and along with the growth of my company, felt rewarding and gave me a sense of accomplishment and purpose.

A few months after my business went into full swing, I decided to explore more of the business world by joining Business Professionals of America. I was encouraged to join just two weeks before the state competition, but I quickly realized it presented an opportunity. I worked for hours every day perfecting my business plan and eight-minute presentation for the entrepreneurship category. Once the day of the competition arrived, I felt immensely proud. Through my commitment to applying the skills I learned by running my business, I placed second out of many. I now feel confident in my abilities to perform strongly in pressure situations and under short deadlines.

After a grueling few years, my mother returned. I realized that sacrifice for following your ideals and helping others, much like my mother did for us, is worth the temporary setbacks. I have taken that message and the incident of watching my parents struggle and am driven to try to succeed in business while helping others. I have gained many strengths through my experiences, the largest of all being my confidence. I noticed it flourishing in myself and my abilities through my work with iCake, BPA, and every other activity I participate in. A once insecure girl who was controlled by her emotions is now empowered.

END.

This essay effectively narrates a journey of personal growth, resilience, and entrepreneurial spirit, driven by family challenges and a passion for baking. Aashika successfully demonstrates how firsthand experiences have translated into business acumen and a keen sense of social responsibility.

INTRODUCTION TO PERSONAL STRUGGLE:

"I was huddled in my room wrapped in many layers of a blanket..."
(The essay starts with a vivid image, setting a tone of vulnerability and a need for comfort in the face of distressing news.)

"...as if desperately longing for comfort from inanimate objects." (This phrase suggests a deep need for security and comfort during a challenging time.)

FAMILY CHALLENGES AND EMOTIONAL IMPACT:

"At ten years old, my brain wasn't prepared for the despondent conversation..." (Indicates the youthful age and unpreparedness of Aashika for serious family issues, emphasizing vulnerability.)

"They were discussing the end of my father's nonprofit, iTforTeens..." (Introduces a pivotal family event that significantly impacts Aashika.)

"My parents floated the possibility of leaving the United States..." (The potential major life change contributes to Aashika's sense of instability and fear.)

PERSONAL STRUGGLES DURING MOTHER'S ABSENCE:

"My mother and I were separated for a few years due to her taking a job..." (Highlights a period of separation, adding to the sense of isolation and emotional struggle.)

"...my body was undergoing changes I didn't want to undergo without the comfort of her arms." (Connects personal developmental challenges with the emotional need for a mother's presence.)

FINDING SOLACE IN BAKING:

"As sweet foods had always brought my mother and me happiness..." (Baking is introduced as a therapeutic activity that connects Aashika to happier memories with her mother.)

"Little treats turned into cakes and cupcakes, and I discovered a strong love for baking..." (Illustrates the evolution of a hobby into a passion, offering refuge from personal challenges.)

BIRTH OF A BUSINESS IDEA:

"As my love for baking grew stronger, an interesting idea crept into my mind." (Signifies the transition from baking as a hobby to a potential business idea.)

"I started a baking business, iCake, which was founded on the philosophy..." (Details the inception of the business and its founding principles, aligning with community support during COVID-19.)

BUSINESS GROWTH AND COMMUNITY IMPACT:

"Making one dozen a week soon intensified to hundreds of cupcakes made and donated." (Demonstrates the rapid growth and scale of the business initiative.)

"Realizing that this was unsustainable for one person, I created a change.org petition..." (Shows problem-solving skills and initiative to expand the impact beyond personal capacity.)

BUSINESS COMPETITION EXPERIENCE:

"A few months after my business went into full swing, I decided to explore more of the business world..." (Indicates a step towards formal business education and experience.)

"I placed second out of many." (Highlights success in a competitive environment, displaying Aashika's ability to learn and excel quickly.)

CONCLUSION AND PERSONAL GROWTH:

"After a grueling few years, my mother returned." (Marks the end of a challenging period and the return of a key family member.)

"I realized that sacrifice for following your ideals and helping others..." (Reflects on the lessons learned from family experiences and personal endeavors.)

"A once insecure girl who was controlled by her emotions is now empowered." (Concludes with a strong statement of personal growth and empowerment, contrasting the beginning of the essay.)

SCRATCH PAPER

SCRATCH PAPER

CHAPTER 10:

Supplemental Essays

SUPPLEMENTAL ESSAYS ARE AN ESSENTIAL tool for colleges to better understand an applicant's suitability for their institution. They allow applicants to demonstrate their interest in the college, articulate how they would contribute to the campus community, and showcase their writing and critical thinking skills.

I prefer to list several essays verbatim from my daughter's college applications as examples. I deliberately did not modify any of them, proving that it is human to err and make minor mistakes. Remember that no matter what, there is always room for improvement, as will be observed through the annotations.

I want to caution parents that they may not find reading someone else's essays exciting or productive but reading someone else's work could be eye-opening for the student.

One of the things to keep in mind is the potential to improve anything written by anyone, so do not feel bad when you get critical feedback on your essays reviewed by someone you trust. There will be minor issues, even if you have made numerous changes and created several drafts, that could be addressed or improved in the essay. The biggest challenge you will encounter is the word limit on the supplemental essays.

By providing annotations, it becomes easier to understand Aashika's intentions, the structure of the essay, and the strategies she used to convey the message and connect with the admissions officer. Wherever possible, I will refer to Aashika as the writer.

1) Describe how you plan to pursue your academic interests and why you want to explore them at USC specifically. Please feel free to address your first- and second-choice major selections. (max 250 words)

The day I'd been simultaneously dreading and anticipating finally arrived. I was shooting for varsity show choir as a sophomore, and the tension held me in a chokehold. As someone who spends most of her time dancing, it felt as if passing this audition would be another milestone proving my dedication to dancing and the weight it has held in my life for over fourteen years. Only five out of forty girls would make it, and the weeks before auditioning were a cycle of practice—practicing just like I would for major performances. My audition passed in a blur of nerves. After weeks of stress, the varsity list came out. Spoiler: I made it, and I spent the following hour sobbing. For me, dance is the gift of expression through movement that I can't live without.

I realized that my passions for business and dance could live together. At USC, I could explore issues of inclusivity and diversity through research opportunities at the Marshall school while taking dance classes in choreography and urban hip-hop at the Kaufman School. Outside the classroom, I intend to pursue leadership positions at ICC and SABA to gain more management experience and help them grow. I'm especially drawn towards the WBB program because it presents well-rounded international exposure at Bocconi and HKUST. Moreover, USC's campus is situated in LA, allowing me to explore the entertainment industry to its fullest and pursue a business career in the performing arts, a life that encompasses both of my passions.

Here are annotations to help you better understand the writing and structure of the essay:

1. The first sentence creates tension and anticipation, a good hook for the reader.

2. The use of the phrase "held me in a chokehold" effectively conveys the writer's anxiety and nervousness.

3. The writer establishes her dedication to dance and its importance in her life, which sets the stage for the rest of the essay.

4. Using the word "spoiler" creates a moment of fun and relief for the reader, which helps to break the tension of the previous paragraph.

5. The writer makes a clear connection between her passion for dance and her academic and career goals at USC, which shows how her experiences and interests have shaped her ambitions.

6. The writer clearly understands the opportunities available at USC and how she can use them to pursue her goals.

7. The writer mentions specific programs and organizations at USC that she is interested in, which shows that she has done her research and is committed to getting involved on campus.

8. The writer makes a compelling case for why USC is the right fit for her and how it can help her achieve her goals.

The essay effectively communicates the writer's passion for dance and how it has shaped her academic and career goals. The essay also shows a clear understanding of the opportunities available at USC and how the writer plans to take advantage of them. The use of specific examples and details helps to make the essay more compelling and persuasive.

While the essay effectively communicates the writer's passion and goals, there are a few potential issues that could be addressed:

The essay is focused primarily on the writer's interests and passions, but it could benefit from more detail about how the writer plans to contribute to the USC community. It would be helpful to mention examples of how the writer intends to get involved on campus and contribute to the USC community.

The writer could also benefit from providing specific examples of how USC's programs and resources will help her achieve her goals. While the essay mentions particular programs like the WBB program, providing more detail about how these programs will benefit would be helpful.

Finally, while the essay is well-written and engaging, it could benefit from editing for clarity and concision. Some sentences are longer than necessary, making the essay dense or complex. By editing for clarity and brevity, the writer could make the essay more accessible and easier to understand.

2) USC faculty place an emphasis on interdisciplinary academic opportunities. Describe something outside of your intended academic focus about which you are interested in learning. (max 250 words)

I have three-and-a-half souls and three-and-a-half ways to perceive the world. I have a Bengali soul, an English, a Hindi, and a half-Marathi soul. This plurality of souls has led to a captivation with the diversity every language holds, the accents and differences and similarities I find within the languages I speak. Three-and-a-half versions of life only languages can give me.

Immersing myself in languages provides a wider peek into the lives of global citizens who live through tasting different words on their tongues every day. Languages eternalize with them so much knowledge; they record how cultures have shaped themselves and will continue to. Learning a language is not merely gaining a second set of words for the world, it is the expansion into a different way of understanding the world. USC offers two of eighteen covered courses open for students to take anything that interests them, and I plan to use them to take language and culture courses in Korean and French, as I am already at elementary proficiency for both. Despite being in a country filled with immigrants, the United States is comparatively linguistically homogeneous, and due to globalization, there is a strong need for incorporating foreign languages in everyday life. Educating ourselves through language learning can change our entire perspective and allow us to revisit the various cultures decorating the US with open minds and in turn, open hearts, to expand our souls.

Below are annotations to help better understand the writing and structure of the essay:

1. Introduction: The writer introduces her unique perspective by stating they have three-and-a-half souls and ways to perceive the world. They also mention their affinity for languages.

2. Language diversity: The writer emphasizes her fascination with linguistic diversity, noting the accents, differences, and similarities within the languages they speak.

3. Importance of languages: The writer explains how languages offer insights into the lives of global citizens and serve as a record of cultural development.

4. Personal experience: The writer mentions her plan to take language and culture courses in Korean and French at USC, which demonstrates their commitment to furthering their linguistic education.

5. Linguistic homogeneity in the U.S.: The writer contrasts the United States' diverse immigrant population with its comparatively homogeneous linguistic landscape.

6. The value of language education: The writer argues that learning languages can change one's perspective, foster a deeper understanding of various cultures, and expand one's soul.

The essay is well-structured, with a clear introduction, a discussion of the writer's personal experience and beliefs regarding language diversity, and a conclusion emphasizing language education's value.

As mentioned, while the essay is well-written and engaging, there are a few areas that the writer could potentially improve:

Clarify the concept of "three-and-a-half souls": The opening statement about having three-and-a-half souls might confuse some readers. Consider elaborating on this idea or rephrasing it to convey the multiple cultural and linguistic identities that shape your perspective more clearly.

Provide specific examples: To make your essay more personal and relatable, include specific examples or anecdotes that illustrate your experiences with language learning and how it has impacted your life. It could consist of a memorable interaction with a native speaker, a challenging linguistic situation, or an insight gained from studying a particular language.

Explain your interest in Korean and French: Mention the reasons behind your interest in learning Korean and French and how gaining proficiency in these languages aligns with your personal, academic, or professional goals.

Discuss USC's unique offerings: Elaborate on why USC's language and culture courses are particularly appealing to you and what aspects of the university's program or environment will support your language learning journey.

Expand on the benefits of language learning: While you mention that language learning can change perspectives and allow for deeper cultural understanding, consider providing more detail on how these benefits could extend to your life or the broader community. For example, you could discuss how language learning promotes cross-cultural communication, fosters empathy, or leads to new opportunities.

By addressing these points and incorporating specific examples, you can further strengthen your essay and provide a more compelling argument for the importance of language learning and your passion for engaging with diverse cultures.

3) What experiences and/or skills best prepare you for success in our World Bachelor in Business program? (max 250 words)

After founding my business and wanting to learn more, I applied and was accepted into three merit-based business camps over the summer. These weeklong camps enabled me to interact with people from all over the world. Before the following school year ended, I was able to attend a program hosted by an eminent entrepreneurial coach from India. I woke up at four a.m. to attend the sessions, and it was eye-opening to communicate with my fellow attendees. I listened to perspectives stemming from their cultural backgrounds and comprehended methods entrepreneurs apply daily.

Throughout my business experiences and leadership positions, my skills have multiplied greatly. From operating my baking business, I gained an understanding of the basics of business management. Along with my entrepreneurial spirit, that experience will give me an edge. Through our school government, I worked to implement my ideas, and through Mentors in Violence Prevention I led freshmen in societal issue conversations. As an Assistant Stage Manager in our theatre program, I co-managed productions. Additionally, show choir allowed me to express myself creatively. My knowledge and affinity for languages will help me navigate other countries and cultures effectively, and I'll even get the chance to explore different cultural dance styles. I strongly feel that studying and working through WBB will support me greatly in accomplishing my professional goals. It will also offer me a robust international alumni network that I can leverage for expanding a business or a global business career.

Here are some annotations to help better understand the writing and structure of the essay:

1. Introduction: The writer briefly introduces her background in business and their desire to learn more through participation in merit-based business camps.

2. International exposure: The writer describes her experience attending a program hosted by an entrepreneurial coach from India and the valuable insights they gained from interacting with fellow attendees from diverse cultural backgrounds.

3. Skills and experiences: The writer enumerates various experiences and leadership positions that have contributed to their personal and professional growth, including running a baking business, participating in school government, and involvement in Mentors in Violence Prevention, theatre, and show choir.

4. Language and cultural competence: The writer emphasizes her knowledge and affinity for languages, which she believes will help her navigate other countries and cultures effectively.

5. WBB program benefits: The writer believes that studying and working through the WBB program will support her professional goals and provide her with a solid international alumni network that she can leverage for business expansion or a global career.

The essay is structured to introduce the writer's background and experiences in business, then detail her various leadership positions and skills gained from those experiences. Next, the writer discusses the importance of language and cultural competence and then explains how the WBB program will contribute to their professional goals.

Here are a few potential points that could be addressed or improved in the essay:

1. Expand on the business camps: Elaborate on the specific business camps attended and the key takeaways from those experiences. Providing concrete examples of the knowledge or skills you gained will help demonstrate your growth and enthusiasm for business.

2. Strengthen connections: Connect your experiences and skills to the WBB program, explaining how they have prepared you for success in the program and how the program will further enhance your abilities.

3. Provide specific professional goals: Mention your specific professional goals, such as starting a global business or working in a particular industry, to clarify how the WBB program will support your aspirations.

4. Maintain focus: While it is essential to mention your diverse experiences, ensure that each experience relates to your central theme – your passion for business and how the WBB program will help you achieve your goals. Be cautious not to deviate too far from the main message.

By addressing these potential issues and making the suggested improvements, the writer can enhance the overall clarity and effectiveness of her essay.

4) How does the WBB program meet your educational and/or professional goals? (max 250 words)

Something important to me is building a sense of community and connections and creating friendships. At USC, there are two organizations I'd be thrilled to join immediately. The South Asian Business

Association will allow me to get to know future businesswomen and men that are part of the same racial group as me, allow me to build business connections in community through shared experiences and perspectives. Additionally, USC MOVE focuses on the intersection between business and social good. The experiences of providing financial support to the University of Iowa Dance Marathon and giving cupcakes to frontline workers through my business have given me the chance to help my community while doing something I love, and USC MOVE will help further that desire, whether it be through hands-on communication with the local community or learning new concepts from professionals.

HKUST and Bocconi also offer fantastic opportunities outside of the classroom. The Entrepreneurship Club and Management & Consulting Club at Bocconi will challenge me to learn how business aspects apply to European countries. The Live Performance Student Association will make space for me to continue my passion for dance. HKUST hosts one of the biggest international case competitions that allow students to interact with and work with peers from all over the world while solving real business cases. Participation in these WBB programs will increase my confidence and give me the chance to meet and compete with the best students all over the world, and in turn, enhance my international network.

Below are some annotations to help better understand the writing and structure of the essay:

1. Introduction: The writer introduces her value for community building, connections, and friendships as a driving force in her interest in extracurricular activities.

2. USC organizations: The writer highlights her desire to join the South Asian Business Association and USC MOVE. She

explains how each organization aligns with their values and interests in building connections within her racial group and combining business with social good.

3. Experiences with community involvement: The writer provides examples of how she has previously contributed to their community through her business, illustrating her commitment to making a positive impact.

4. Bocconi opportunities: The writer discusses her interest in Bocconi's Entrepreneurship Club and Management & Consulting Club, as well as the Live Performance Student Association, which aligns with her passion for dance.

5. HKUST case competition: The writer mentions her excitement about participating in international case competitions at HKUST, emphasizing the opportunity to collaborate with and learn from peers worldwide.

6. Benefits of WBB program participation: The writer concludes by expressing her belief that engaging in these activities across the WBB programs will boost their confidence, expand their international network, and allow her to connect with top students worldwide.

The essay is structured first to introduce the writer's values and then explore the specific opportunities they are excited about at each institution mentioned (USC, Bocconi, and HKUST). By detailing how each opportunity aligns with her interests and goals, the writer effectively communicates her enthusiasm and commitment to making the most of her educational experience.

While the essay effectively highlights enthusiasm for community building and extracurricular activities, there are a few things that can be improved:

1. Elaborate on the impact of the activities: Explain how participating in the mentioned activities will contribute to your personal, academic, or professional growth. Providing specific examples of the skills you hope to gain or the experiences you expect to have will help illustrate the importance of these opportunities.

2. Discuss your contributions: Share how your experiences and skills will enable you to contribute to these organizations and activities. It will demonstrate that you will be an active and valuable community member.

Addressing these points and providing more context and clarity can further strengthen the essay and create a more compelling argument for your participation in the WBB program and the associated opportunities.

5) What skills do you find most useful in adapting to changing environments? (max 250 words)

I experienced my solo introduction to the world when I went to live with my grandparents over the summer a few years ago. I've always been self-conscious of my American accent pushing through every word I speak in Bengali and Hindi, so when my grandma asked me in Bengali to buy her groceries from the vendor down the street, I was frantic. I could speak Hindi to get the groceries, but it sounded so foreign. I knew that I would have to do this because I couldn't make my grandma do it herself. I practiced a few times to make sure I would be understood and thought through how I'd get there. I traveled down the apartment stairs and quickly pushed through the crowded lane in Surat, nearly out of breath. I used my Hindi skills and a few hand gestures to buy everything needed but didn't declare victory until the confines of the flat surrounded me.

Confidence is the most important skill to have when experiencing changing environments. Once you can find the confidence to tackle a situation that's out of your comfort zone, skill development follows. I used verbal and non-verbal communication when buying groceries, and this will occur in the WBB program as we travel to places with different languages. Additionally, taking time to learn the basics of a new language and day-to-day life in a new environment is essential to adapting quickly. Ultimately, gaining knowledge about the area will boost self-confidence and lead to success.

Here is the annotation of the essay with specific keywords to illustrate the structure:

1. Solo introduction: The essay opens with the writer's "solo introduction to the world" when living with their grandparents, setting the stage for a personal story about overcoming language barriers.

2. Self-consciousness: The writer shares her self-consciousness about their "American accent" in Bengali and Hindi, revealing vulnerability and connecting with the reader.

3. Grandma's request: The writer describes her "frantic" reaction when asked to buy groceries in Bengali, highlighting her challenge and determination to overcome it.

4. Taking action: The writer details her preparation, practicing their Hindi and navigating the crowded streets of Surat, demonstrating her problem-solving skills and adaptability.

5. Grocery shopping success: The writer recounts her successful use of Hindi and hand gestures to complete the task, conveying a sense of accomplishment and personal growth.

6. Confidence and skill development: The essay transitions to a broader lesson about the importance of confidence in adapting to new environments and how skill development follows.

7. Connection to WBB program: The writer relates her personal experience to the WBB program, emphasizing the value of verbal and non-verbal communication, learning new languages, and adapting to new environments for success.

The above points highlight the key elements of the essay's structure and writing, providing a better understanding of the narrative and its connection to the writer's experience and future goals.

While the essay is engaging and effectively conveys the writer's personal experience, there are a few areas that could potentially be improved:

1. More precise connection to the WBB program: Although the essay mentions the WBB program and how the writer's experience relates to it, the reference could be made more explicit. The writer could elaborate on specific aspects of the program that align with their experience and how these aspects will contribute to her growth.

2. More examples of adaptability: The writer could provide additional examples of how she has adapted to new environments or faced challenges in the past. It would help reinforce the adaptability theme and show a growth and resilience pattern.

3. Personal reflection: The essay could benefit from a deeper reflection on how the experience shaped the writer's

perspective and changed her approach to facing challenges. It would add depth and introspection to the narrative.

4. Broader implications: The writer could discuss the wider implications of their experience, such as the importance of cultural understanding or how learning to adapt can lead to personal and professional success.

The writer can strengthen the essay by addressing these potential improvements to offer a more comprehensive insight into her experiences, personal growth, and connection to the WBB program.

6) Acknowledging that the WBB does not offer a "traditional" or fixed residential experience, please explain why this alternative education experience is a good fit for you. Please share examples of how you plan to create unique or new opportunities in the WBB environment. (max 250 words)

The internet constantly exposes the world's beauty to us, and with it comes my desire to travel. I am, simply put, obsessed with visiting new places. Since childhood, studying abroad has been first on my college "to accomplish" list. I've been lucky enough to visit eight countries on four different continents, eight new cultures I've been exposed to and learned from. As I started connecting with current WBB students, I've learned so much from their experiences that compel me to pursue my own.

At USC Marshall I'd have the opportunity to engage with the Hollywood industry and potentially meet notable people in the industry, as the business aspect of entertainment is what I want to pursue. While at Bocconi, I can learn about financing related to moviemaking and even become part of Movision Film Productions as a way to experiment with my dual interest and learn about how business is incorporated in unexpected ways behind the big screen. As part of WBB, HKUST encourages students to take humanities courses alongside their core competencies and this could be an excellent opportunity to learn about the technological aspect of the Asian film industry. Incredible works like Parasite, Spirited Away, and Internal Affairs (which took place in Hong Kong!) have piqued my interest in East Asian cinema specifically. The travel aspect of WBB will help me gain a holistic world approach to business in the cinematic/performing arts and allow me to employ my knowledge no matter where in the world I settle.

This collection of interpretative notes aims to enhance the reading experience by shedding light on the essay's structural and rhetorical strategies.

1. Travel and exposure: The essay opens with the writer's fascination with traveling and experiencing novel places, setting the context for their desire to study abroad.

2. Childhood goal: The writer shares that studying abroad has always been a priority on their college "to accomplish" list, emphasizing the importance of international experiences.

3. Connecting with WBB students: The writer mentions connecting with current WBB students, showing their initiative to learn from others, and further solidifying their interest in the program.

4. USC Marshall opportunities: The essay details potential engagement with the Hollywood industry and meeting notable people, reflecting the writer's interest in the business side of entertainment.

5. Bocconi and film financing: The writer discusses learning about film financing at Bocconi and joining Movision Film

Productions, highlighting her desire to explore the intersection of business and entertainment.

6. HKUST humanities courses: The essay highlights HKUST's emphasis on humanities courses and the opportunity to learn about the technological aspect of the Asian film industry, demonstrating the writer's interest in East Asian cinema.

7. Holistic world approach: The writer concludes by explaining how the WBB program's travel aspect will help them gain a global perspective on the cinematic and performing arts business, enabling them to apply their knowledge anywhere they settle.

These notes provide an overview of the essay's structure and key points, helping to understand the writer's interest in the WBB program and their passion for combining business with the entertainment industry.

The essay is engaging and effective. However, there are a few areas that could potentially be improved:

1. Personal experiences: The writer could provide more specific individual experiences or anecdotes related to their passion for traveling, learning about diverse cultures, or their interest in the business aspect of the entertainment industry. It would help the reader better understand the writer's motivations and background.

2. Elaborate on WBB's impact: The writer could discuss in more detail how the WBB program will uniquely contribute to her personal and professional growth, as well as the

specific skills and experiences she hopes to gain from each of the universities involved in the program.

3. Extracurricular involvement: The writer could mention any relevant extracurricular activities, internships, or projects she has undertaken that demonstrate their commitment to the entertainment industry and her ability to succeed in the WBB program.

4. Long-term goals: The essay could benefit from a more precise explanation of the writer's long-term career goals and how the WBB program will help them achieve them. It would help demonstrate the writer's focus and drive and the program's role in her future success.

By addressing these potential improvements, the essay can provide a more comprehensive insight into the writer's passion for the entertainment industry, her experiences, and how the WBB program will contribute to their personal and professional growth.

For the following UT Austin essays, I will change my format of providing in-text annotations. Also, I am not going to leave suggestions for improvements. It is deliberate because I want you to make notes on what you think can be improved after reading the merits of the essays.

7) Why are you interested in the major you indicated as your first choice major? (max 300 words)

I've been surrounded by entrepreneurs my entire life. My father was a partner in an IT business for 14 years before selling off his stake. After that, he founded a non-profit organization called iTforTeens in which I was able to observe and volunteer. Moreover, three of my uncles in India are entrepreneurs who own businesses. I hadn't thought seriously about pursuing a career in business, but while quarantined during the pandemic, I was able to turn my baking passion into a business opportunity. iCake was born from my kitchen in September of 2020. Support from my community and positive customer feedback encouraged me to invest several hours a week into my business. Being CEO has shaped me as a businesswoman. I wear multiple hats in terms of sales, marketing, and operations, and I've grasped customer emotions and what customer delight really means. I've learned to handle challenging situations patiently and with empathy. iCake has taught me many leadership skills including decision making and strategic thinking. Some concepts I now understand are product pricing, product positioning, product upselling, and product cross-selling.

Through my learning, I discovered an interest in marketing going hand-in-hand with entrepreneurship. Leveraging Facebook advertising as a marketing tool was the catalyst for my marketing curiosity. Additionally, Business Professionals of America through high school has been one of my favorite school activities. It's given me even more opportunities to learn about business management and practice public speaking. While actively running my business and maintaining membership of BPA, I've found something that I thoroughly enjoy and can certainly see myself doing in the future. The confidence and communication skills I've learned through combining my family's entrepreneurial spirit with my culinary skills motivate me to pursue my interest in this remarkable field.

Introduction to Entrepreneurial Background:

- "I've been surrounded by entrepreneurs my entire life."
  (Here, the writer begins by establishing a personal connection to the field of entrepreneurship, emphasizing the influence of their familial background on their interest in business.)

Family's Influence:

- "My father was a partner in an IT business for 14 years…"
  (The writer provides specific examples of entrepreneurial
  influences within their family, grounding their interest in
  real-life observations and experiences.)

  "Moreover, three of my uncles in India are entrepreneurs who
  own businesses." (This further solidifies the extent of their exposure
  to entrepreneurship, expanding the influence on a global context.)

Personal Entrepreneurial Experience - iCake:

- "I hadn't thought seriously about pursuing a career in business, but…" (Here, the writer introduces a turning point in
  her journey, shifting from observation to active participation in the field.)
- "iCake was born from my kitchen in September of 2020."
  (The inception of her personal business venture is highlighted, adding a practical dimension to her interest in
  entrepreneurship.)

Learning and Development Through iCake:

- "Being CEO has shaped me as a businesswoman." (The
  writer reflects on her growth and the skills she has developed through running her own business.)
- "I've learned to handle challenging situations patiently and
  with empathy." (This demonstrates her ability to adapt and
  develop essential leadership skills.)

Discovery of Interest in Marketing:

- "Through my learning, I discovered an interest in marketing going hand-in-hand with entrepreneurship." (The writer identifies a specific area within the business that has captured her interest, providing direction for her academic pursuits.)
- "Leveraging Facebook advertising as a marketing tool was the catalyst for my marketing curiosity." (She offers a concrete example of how her entrepreneurial venture led her to explore marketing, demonstrating an applied understanding of the field.)

Involvement in Business Professionals of America (BPA):

- "Additionally, Business Professionals of America through high school has been one of my favorite school activities." (The writer mentions another platform through which she has explored her interest in business, displaying her proactive approach to learning.)
- "It's given me even more opportunities to learn about business management and practice public speaking." (This highlights the skills and knowledge she gained through her involvement in BPA.)

Conclusion and Future Aspirations:

- "The confidence and communication skills I've learned through combining my family's entrepreneurial spirit with my culinary skills motivate me to pursue my interest in this remarkable field." (The writer ties together her familial influences, individual experiences, and acquired skills to express a solid motivation to continue exploring business and marketing in the future.)

8) Describe how your experiences, perspectives, talents, and/or your involvement and leadership activities (at your school, job, community, or within your family) will help you to make an impact both in and out of the classroom while enrolled at UT. (max 300 words)

The beat of my heart drummed so loudly I could barely hear my voice above my nerves. Twenty pairs of eyes stared at me as I began to tell the contestants about my business and baking experience while providing tips and tricks. By the end of the five minutes that felt like hours, I knew my audience had learned a few things and prepared to trust my judgment. I had been invited by the Iowa City Public Library to judge a cupcake contest ending with my stomach exploding with the delicious flavors of lemon, chocolate, strawberry, and caramel. Each baker had a unique flavor and design to impress me. I still remember the small girl with her panda design, one of the cutest and most professional-looking cupcakes I have ever seen. Getting together with other teens enthusiastic about baking was an incredible experience and led me to look into organizations where I can find a similar home during college.

This is why I feel that joining the UT Austin Meal Movement is a great fit for me. It aligns with my philanthropic ideals and focuses on hands-on cooking and teaching experiences. Through this organization, I would like to become a mentor and impart my own baking knowledge while also mastering additional cooking skills from others.

In addition to baking, my second passion is dance. My journey as an Indian classical Kathak dancer since the age of three has taken me through various fundraising performances while exploring different dance styles. Nritya Sangam is a dance team at UT Austin where I can dive deeper into classical dancing, experience dance fusion, and teach others the beauty of expression through movement while continuing to do what I love.

Introduction to Personal Experience:

- "The beat of my heart drummed so loudly..." (The essay begins with a vivid and emotional description of a moment of personal challenge and achievement, setting a tone of authenticity and engagement.)

Experience as a Judge in a Baking Contest:

- "Twenty pairs of eyes stared at me as I began to tell..." (The writer describes a specific experience where she was placed in a position of authority and expertise, demonstrating her ability to handle pressure and responsibility.)
- "I had been invited by the Iowa City Public Library..." (This highlights an external recognition of the writer's skills and experience, adding credibility to her story.)

Interaction with Young Bakers:

- "Each baker had a unique flavor and design to impress me." (The writer reflects on the diversity of talents and creativity she witnessed, showing appreciation for individuality.)
- "I still remember the small girl with her panda design..." (A particular moment is shared to underscore the impact of this experience on the writer, highlighting her attention to detail and capacity for empathy.)

Connection to UT Austin Meal Movement:

- "This is why I feel that joining the UT Austin Meal Movement is a great fit for me." (The writer directly connects her past experiences and a specific organization at UT Austin, demonstrating intentionality in her choice of college activities.)

- "Through this organization, I would like to become a mentor…" (She desires to contribute and impact, showing a forward-thinking and community-oriented mindset.)

Passion for Dance and Connection to Nritya Sangam:

- "In addition to baking, my second passion is dance." (The essay transitions to another area of interest and expertise, providing a well-rounded view of the writer's talents and passions.)

- "Nritya Sangam is a dance team at UT Austin where I can dive deeper…" (Similar to the previous connection, the writer identifies a specific group at UT Austin where she can continue pursuing her passions and contributing.)

9) The core purpose of The University of Texas at Austin is, To Transform Lives for the Benefit of Society. Please share how you believe your experience at UT-Austin will prepare you to Change the World after you graduate. (max 300 words)

While responding to this prompt, I feel that I am guaranteed a life-changing student experience at UT Austin, which will be transformative. I am currently involved in "Change[ing] my Community" as a volunteer baker. I have been able to honor frontline workers with cupcake donations throughout the pandemic. As a philanthropist, my business has been able to provide monetary support to the UI Dance

Marathon that helps young cancer patients and their families. One of my prized possessions is a recent thank you letter I received from Lynette L. Marshall, President and CEO of the University of Iowa Foundation. This kind of positive impact is what I hope to continue through my association with UT Austin.

UT Austin has drawn me in because of the Canfield Business Honors Program. Some of the main attractions are small class sizes of 30 to 40 students, a small cohort of 100 to 120 students, and a curriculum modeled after case-based MBA programs. Students are paired with a personal Career Coach in their first semester and there are opportunities to work with the alumni mentor network and chances to work with the Board of Regions for budgets/tuition. Opportunities for doing compelling research are offered, like how diversity and inclusion affect Mergers & Acquisitions, a topic in business I'm interested in. My membership with the Technology Association of Iowa exposed me to the disparity of women in business, a cause close to my heart. I would love to join the McCombs Diversity Council and Women in Business Association at UT Austin to encourage more women of color in business.

Introduction and Overview of Personal Involvement:

- "While responding to this prompt..." (The writer establishes her awareness of the transformative potential at UT Austin and sets a confident tone about her readiness to contribute.)

Current Community Impact through Baking:

- "I am currently involved in 'Change[ing] my Community' as a volunteer baker..." (The writer provides specific examples of her current contributions to her community, demonstrating her commitment to service and societal benefit.)

Connection with the Canfield Business Honors Program:

- "UT Austin has drawn me in because of the Canfield Business Honors Program." (The writer directly connects her aspirations and a specific program at UT Austin, showcasing research and intention in their application.)
- "Some of the main attractions are small class sizes..." (Detailing specific program features illustrates the writer's thorough understanding and genuine interest in what the program offers.)

Career Development and Research Opportunities:

- "Students are paired with a personal Career Coach..." (Mentioning this resource shows the writer's anticipation of utilizing the available support for their professional growth.)
- "Opportunities for doing compelling research are offered..." (The writer is eager to engage in academic inquiry, pointing out specific areas of interest.)

Advocacy for Women in Business:

- "My membership with the Technology Association of Iowa exposed me to the disparity of women in business..." (The essay reflects the writer's awareness of gender disparities in her field of interest and her commitment to addressing this issue.)

- "I would love to join the McCombs Diversity Council and Women in Business Association..." (Identifying specific groups at UT Austin demonstrates the writer's proactive attitude and intention to continue her advocacy work.)

Conclusion:

- In this essay, the writer has successfully conveyed her commitment to societal transformation through personal and community involvement and has connected her aspirations with specific programs and opportunities at UT Austin. She has also highlighted her interest in research and advocacy, demonstrating a well-rounded and thoughtful approach to how she intends to "Change the World" after graduation.

10) Forty Acres Scholars participate in valuable programming and attend many events throughout their four years on campus. Examples include: a weekly Freshman Dinner Series in the fall of their first semester, an annual retreat, service opportunities, the Distinguished Alumnus Awards, and Forty Acres Discussions with prominent UT alumni. If you were selected to be a Forty Acres Scholar, what programming event would you look forward to the most? Additionally, what programming ideas do you have that could benefit the Forty Acres Scholars Program? (max 300 words)

"Once upon a time, there lived five brothers called Pandavas in the city of Indraprastha," my grandmother began as my 7-year-old frame glued to her with excitement. There was a competitive Swayamvara contest for Princess Draupadi to choose her husband. The test was to lift and string a bow and then fire arrows to pierce the eye of a golden fish only by looking at its reflection in the water. At the Swayamvara, no monarch was able to complete the challenge besides a Pandava brother named Arjuna who succeeded in the end. He then wed Draupadi, the most beautiful woman of the time. "That is the basis of the Arjuna award," concluded my grandmother as we watched it unfold on TV during an annual trip to India. The award is named after Arjuna, one of the central characters of the Sanskrit epic Mahabharata of ancient India. Since then, award ceremonies have always captured my attention with the Oscars, Emmys, and Grammys being annual rituals in our household.

Attending the Distinguished Alumnus Awards would be my first choice. Consuming the motivational speeches and the words of wisdom laced with interesting stories from the speakers' lives would be captivating for a young Longhorn. Being able to listen to Governor Greg Abbott's grand story of the 1969 game between Texas and Arkansas where he goes on to say, "What matters is not how much you are down but how you come back," is mind-blowing!

The icing on the cake would be an opportunity to participate in a live performance in between speakers or help add them to make the ceremony more festive. Since choir, show choir, and theatre have been integral parts of my high school universe, adding a little bit of me to the vibrant celebration would be a wish fulfilled.

Introduction (Lines 1-3):

- The writer opens with a personal anecdote about Indian culture, immediately establishing a unique perspective and providing context for her interest in award ceremonies.
- The use of a childhood story makes the introduction engaging and sets a narrative tone for the essay.

Connection to the Prompt (Lines 4-5):

- The writer smoothly transitions from the personal anecdote to the subject of award ceremonies, linking her childhood fascination to her current interests.

- By mentioning specific, well-known award ceremonies (Oscars, Emmys, Grammys), the writer demonstrates her genuine interest in such events.

Specific Interest in Forty Acres Programming (Lines 6-9):

- The writer clearly states that attending the Distinguished Alumnus Awards is her programming event of choice, directly addressing the prompt.

- She expresses enthusiasm about gaining inspiration from speeches and stories shared by accomplished alumni, highlighting a desire for personal growth and learning.

Personal Engagement and Contribution (Lines 10-11):

- The essay shifts to express a secret desire to contribute to the event, suggesting involvement in live performances.

- This section demonstrates the writer's eagerness to participate in programming and contribute and actively enhance the experience for others.

Closing Statement (Line 12):

- The essay concludes by tying back to the writer's high school experiences, reinforcing her passion for performance and her desire to share this aspect of herself with the community.

- The phrase "wish fulfilled" leaves a positive, aspirational tone, suggesting that being a part of such events would be a dream come true for the writer.

Overall Structure and Content:

- The essay successfully combines a personal narrative, a direct response to the prompt, and a forward-looking desire to contribute, providing a well-rounded answer. The unique and engaging narrative style helps the essay stand out, and the clear connection to the programming event adds relevance and coherence.

11) As the only program of its kind administered by an alumni association, the Forty Acres Scholars Program fosters a unique connection between Scholars and alumni. Scholars build relationships with alumni and leave campus with an impressive and supportive network. How has your life been enriched by mentors so far? And what specifically do you hope to gain from the vast Texas Exes network? (max 300 words) [Teacher's name changed to maintain privacy]

Mrs. Smith's face lit with joy when she heard that I had started a baking business in the middle of a pandemic. As she spoke, I could sense the presence of a proud parent with words of encouragement patting me on the back and I was elated with an air of confidence. It was the moment I was sucked into her club, Business Professionals of America. Just a few months into the membership, I was reaping the benefits with a second-place entrepreneurship award at the Iowa State Conference competition. The gift of mentorship was handed to me by Mrs. Smith and her endless advice leading up to the event.

It was at that pivotal point I realized how lucky I have been to have several teachers since childhood acting as mentors, offering a perspective that is often hard to find otherwise. They weren't afraid to challenge my ideas or create discomfort of thoughts, mirroring a similar atmosphere at home. At UT Austin, I will be looking for a "Guru" (Sanskrit: "venerable"). According to the ancient Indian scriptures of "Vedas", the guru who, though human, has achieved spiritual enlightenment and thus leads the devotee to discover the same potentialities within themselves.

Meeting Gary Kelly would be a full circle for me since I have heard so much about my mother's chance encounter with Mr. Kelly during her stint at Southwest Airlines. My mother had raving reviews about their work culture, especially the unique and inviting Monday night deck parties and the encouraging atmosphere contributing to stronger engagement and wellness. Besides exchanging ideas and seeking his advice and blessings, I'd want to ask Mr. Kelly about his weekly parties and the road to success. Honestly, I'm expecting the Texas Exec network to be my friend, philosopher, and guide, just like Mrs. Smith.

Introduction (Lines 1-3):

- Personal Experience with Mentorship: The writer starts with a vivid description of a pivotal moment with a mentor, Mrs. Smith, highlighting the positive impact and confidence gained from the mentorship. [Creating a strong emotional connection and highlighting the importance of mentorship in the writer's life.]
- Connection to the Prompt: By sharing this story, the writer immediately addresses the first part of the prompt, discussing how mentors have enriched her life. [Ensuring

relevance to the prompt and setting the stage for a comprehensive answer.]

Middle Section (Lines 4-7):

- Expansion on Mentorship Experience: The essay elaborates on the impact of mentorship, sharing a specific achievement attributed to Mrs. Smith's guidance. [Providing concrete evidence of the benefits of mentorship.]

- Reflection on Past Mentorships: The writer shares a realization about mentors' consistent presence and value throughout her life, linking this to her family environment. [Adding depth to their understanding of mentorship and creating a seamless transition to the next part of the essay.]

Connection to Future Aspirations (Lines 8-9):

- Looking Forward at UT Austin: The writer expresses her intention to seek out a mentor at UT Austin, referencing cultural and historical concepts of mentorship. [Demonstrating cultural awareness and a deep appreciation for mentorship.]

- Detailed Expectations: By defining what a "Guru" means to her, the writer sets specific expectations for the type of mentorship she seeks. [Providing clarity on what she is looking for in a mentor at UT Austin.]

Specific Goals with Texas Exes Network (Lines 10-13):

- Personal Connection to Texas Exes: The writer shares a personal story about her mother's experience with a notable UT alum, creating a tangible connection to the Texas

Exes network. [Building a bridge between her personal history and the Texas Exes network.]

- Expressing Specific Expectations: The essay concludes by explicitly stating what the writer hopes to gain from the Texas Exes network, comparing it to the mentorship received from Mrs. Smith. [Directly addressing the second part of the prompt and tying back to the initial story.]

Overall Structure and Content:

- The essay successfully intertwines personal experiences with future aspirations, providing a well-rounded response to the prompt. Using vivid storytelling, personal connections, and clear expectations creates an engaging and insightful narrative.

12) Each Forty Acres Scholar receives a $13,000 enrichment stipend to use toward a global experience such as study abroad, research, service and volunteering, or an internship. If you are selected, how would you spend these funds? (max 300 words)

I've always been highly passionate about studying abroad, so I would spend these funds traveling to either France or Italy to study and participate in a research project. Because it's a global experience, my first choice of project would be involvement in research related to comparing certain aspects of companies or conducting consulting research across continents or Europe. Additionally, I could explore issues of inclusivity and diversity in the workplace through these research opportunities as well, and compare them with the United States to help find ways to make our culture's occupations foster kinder environments for all.

Apart from the research itself, the opportunity to manage work-life balance in a different country and be more independent while living away from UT Austin excites me, especially now as I transition into adulthood. I'm also curious about what to expect from the work environment and professors, as it will be more of a real-world experience. Above all, I strive to learn about various cultural aspects and enjoy the company of locals while conversing in their language and chowing down on delicious meals. It would be even more fulfilling to visit smaller towns and see local hidden gems and national treasures.

Additionally, these funds would allow chances to job shadow or intern with alums and large companies across the globe to garner work experience before graduation. As someone who wants to travel and aspires to own her own company someday, encountering day-to-day professional life in other countries and even in the United States would give me in-person experience and help me accomplish my goals sooner. Becoming a part of the 40 Acres Scholarship Program will not only aid in teaching me life skills at an accelerated rate, but overall will change who I am as a person as I achieve my dreams.

Introduction and Study Abroad Aspirations:

- "I've always been highly passionate about studying abroad..." (The writer sets a clear and enthusiastic tone, expressing an ardent desire for international experience.)

- "...so I would spend these funds traveling to either France or Italy to study and participate in a research project." (She provides specific countries of interest, which adds a level of detail and shows she has thought about her choices.)

Research Interests and Cultural Objectives:

- "Because it's a global experience, my first choice of project..." (The writer emphasizes her interest in global experiences, showcasing a broad perspective.)

- "...comparing certain aspects of companies or conducting consulting research across continents or Europe." (She articulates specific research interests, demonstrating that they have considered how to make the most of this opportunity.)

- "Additionally, I could explore issues of inclusivity and diversity in the workplace..." (Here, the writer introduces a socially relevant and significant topic, aligning her personal interests with broader societal issues.)

Personal Growth and Independence:

- "Apart from the research itself, the opportunity to manage work-life balance..." (She reflects on personal development and understands the broader benefits of studying abroad.)

- "I'm also curious about what to expect from the work environment and professors..." (Expressing curiosity, the writer shows an eagerness to learn and adapt to new environments.)

Networking and Career Development:

- "Additionally, these funds would allow chances to job shadow or intern..." (The essay discusses practical, career-oriented opportunities made possible by the stipend.)

- "As someone who wants to travel and aspires to own her own company someday..." (The writer links the opportunity to her long-term goals, demonstrating foresight and ambition.)

Reflection on the Forty Acres Scholars Program:

- "Becoming a part of the 40 Acres Scholarship Program will not only aid in teaching me life skills..." (The writer concludes by reflecting on the transformative potential of the program, tying back to her personal and professional aspirations.)

Conclusion:

- The essay effectively outlines how the writer would utilize the $13,000 enrichment stipend, providing a well-rounded plan that includes academic pursuits and personal development. She has connected her research and global experience interests with her long-term goals, demonstrating a thoughtful and ambitious approach. Additionally, she has shown an appreciation for the broader benefits of the Forty Acres Scholars Program, highlighting its potential impact on her growth and achievement of her dreams.

These examples from my daughter's real college applications for USC and UT Austin provide ample examples and guidance on presenting your thoughts and ideas in your essays. Admissions officers try to understand who you are and what you stand for in this section. I told Aashika to be as creative as a storyteller when weaving a compelling narrative. I had advised her to think about the narrative in her favorite books and the writing style of her favorite authors and channel those in her essay writing. Manifesting a favorite author can influence the results you seek in essays.

SCRATCH PAPER

CHAPTER 11:

If you don't ask, you don't get

YOU SHOULD REACH OUT TO as many people as you can so that you can tell your story. Once you tell them that, people will only know the importance of what you may have accomplished. You need to be able to highlight what you have done through social media and traditional media. It will help underscore that your accomplishments have been validated by other people, thereby lending a certain level of legitimacy. Again, reaching out to people without any hesitation is critical to success. Identifying people you need to contact might be overwhelming at first, but once you start figuring this out, finding people you need to network with will be easier.

As I had alluded to before, parents play a huge role. They should assist their children in whatever capacity they can to share the burden between the parents and the students in this endeavor. I will publish several emails from my bucket to emphasize this idea of collaboration with your child with a shared goal in mind.

Instead of writing paragraph after paragraph, I will pick a handful of emails I had sent as a parent that helped my daughter get in front of the right people. It also includes some responses I received to my emails.

Sat, Jan 23, 2021, 11:48 AM

to me ▾

Hi Mr. Praveen

I read through Aashika's profile and article, and it makes me so happy reading about her business. I would love to interview her. I shall email you the questions for her in a while as i am preoccupied with work. She can answer them via email itself whenever she feels comfortable. I'm sure m readers would love to read about fellow teenagers doing such work and reaching such heights.

Would be looking forward to hearing from you.

Thanks a lot.

Jan 31, 2021, 4:58 PM

to me ▾

Hi Praveen! Thanks for your message, your daughter sounds amazing. If she'd like I would love to have a Zoom call with her. I started The _____ when I was 19 and would love to chat with her entrepreneur to entrepreneur.

Let me know and I can have my team schedule!

CEO & Founder

Forbes | WWD

Here is one from my side that attempts to leverage the school district newsletter for highlighting my daughter's accomplishment.

Praveen Gadkari <gadkaripraveen@gmail.com>
to _____ ▾

Hi _____,

Thanks for the newsletter... I saw a section about SHOUT-OUT TO OUR STUDENTS, which was inspiring and that made me wonder about the kind of students you pick to feature under this section! The reason is that, at least in my opinion, my daughter Aashika Gadkari has an inspiring story of entrepreneurship. She started a successful baking business as a junior, in September 2020 from our kitchen. Please check her FB page out at https://www.facebook.com/iCakebyAashika/

Additionally, through her business she has been bringing smiles and honoring frontline workers/heroes fighting Covid-19 by giving cupcakes.

Aashika can provide more details if you want to hear from her!

Thanks in advance,
Praveen Gadkari

Here is another one that investigates the idea of self-nomination for an award if the high school did not consider Aashika as part of their submission.

Fwd: Hills Bank Youth Salute Nominations   » Inbox x

Anita Gadkari   Mon, Mar 29, 2021, 3:46 PM   ☆
--------- Forwarded message --------- From: ▇▇▇▇▇▇▇▇▇▇@iowacityschools.org> Date: Mon, Mar 29, 2021 at 3:23 PM Subject: Hil...

Praveen Gadkari <gadkari.praveen@gmail.com>   Tue, Mar 30, 2021, 1:52 PM   ☆ ↩ ⋮
to ▇▇▇▇▇▇▇, Anita ▾
Hi ▇▇,

Hope all is well... I was wondering about this nomination for Aashika.   I am not sure if the school was planning to nominate her or if she should self nominate as suggested by the email below.

Any thoughts?

Thanks,
Praveen

The next one is addressed to a local newspaper.

17 year old Entrepreneur leading Change.org campaign to honor frontline   ✕ 🖶 ☒
workers!   » Inbox x

Praveen Gadkari <gadkari.praveen@gmail.com>   Apr 23, 2021, 4:30 PM   ☆ ↩ ⋮
to ▇▇▇▇ ▾
Hi ▇▇▇,

My 17 year old daughter (Iowa City West High Junior) is the CEO/Owner of iCake and a Hills Bank Leadership Grant Program Winner.

Aashika Gadkari is currently leading a https://www.change.org/HonorFrontlineWorkers campaign to honor our frontline heroes. She is the youngest member of the Technology Association of Iowa to be invited to attend their startup roundtable. Additionally and most importantly, Aashika's desire to get out of her comfort zone with the boldness of attempting new things is demonstrated by being selected as one of the state finalists for the coveted title of Miss Iowa Teen USA in Des Moines over the forthcoming summer.

I sincerely hope that this uncommon student gets some news coverage so that her change.org campaign becomes successful.

Thanks in advance,
Praveen Gadkari

The congratulatory email below is in response to a nomination I had submitted.

KCRG-TV9 Student of the Month - Aashika Gadkari ⟫ Inbox x   ↕ 🖨 ☑

⬛⬛⬛⬛⬛⬛⬛⬛⬛⬛⬛⬛⬛⬛   Tue, May 4, 2021, 8:42AM   ☆ ↰ ⋮
to aashikagadkari@gmail.com, me, ⬛⬛⬛ ▾

Good Morning Aashika,

My name is ⬛⬛⬛⬛⬛⬛ and I am an anchor at KCRG-TV9 in Cedar Rapids. I am emailing to congratulate you on being selected as the KCRG-TV9 Student of the Month for May!

As part of being the May Student of the Month, we will need to arrange a time for an on-camera interview with you, Aashika. Would we be able to meet at your home, to get some video of you doing your schoolwork as well as you decorating cakes or baking for your business?

If so, are you available sometime for an hour either next Monday, Tuesday, or Wednesday (May 10, 11, or 12)?

Mr. ⬛⬛⬛, would you be available for an on-camera interview at Iowa City West High?

Thank you for your time, and I look forward to hearing from you.

Congratulations again!

⬛⬛⬛⬛

Here is one that I had sent to a local business journal. My goal was to get an article published that would put a spotlight on Aashika

Young Entrepreneur ⟫ Inbox x   ↕ 🖨 ☑

Praveen Gadkari <gadkaripraveeni@gmail.com>   Sun, Dec 13, 2020, 4:11 PM   ☆ ↰ ⋮
to ⬛⬛⬛⬛⬛⬛, Anita ▾

Hi ⬛⬛⬛⬛⬛,

Hope all is well...

I am wondering if CBJ is interested in profiling my 16-year-old daughter, Aashika Gadkari, who happens to be a budding entrepreneur. I am proud to state that she started her baking business earlier this year, called ICake (https://www.facebook.com/ICake-104921471370086/). She is a junior at West High, who likes to indulge in her passion for baking during her free time for fulfilling numerous cake orders every week

You could potentially start a 20 under 20 someday!!!

Thanks,
Praveen Gadkari

The main message in this chapter is parental involvement and commitment towards their child's success. These emails (and there were many more) demonstrate that a parent can do many things to identify opportunities and people besides establishing communication with them as the first point of contact and, in some ways, as the first line of defense. This tactical strategy is crucial and pivotal in the shared college admissions journey.

I am not suggesting that parents take complete ownership of the brand building (after all, that is what it is) for their child. As reiterated earlier, this should be considered a shared endeavor with a common goal. It should be an easy decision to think that parental involvement is a huge motivator for the child as they know they have another pillar of strength besides their teachers and counselors.

SCRATCH PAPER

CHAPTER 12:

Common Data Set and Generative AI

In my view, Generative AI has taken our world by storm. Any discussion would be complete with mentioning the power of that force. The idea is to introduce this tool to our readers so that they can leverage it to their benefit. I will show you specific examples of using it in this chapter. Think of ChatGPT as your virtual assistant or a thought leader, and start by asking relevant questions, known as prompts. A lot has already been written about "Prompt Engineering" to enable asking well-designed questions and iterating on the answers until getting appropriate answers. The trick is to treat tools like ChatGPT or Bard as an expert in the subject you are researching or ideating.

I've yet to discuss a nifty nugget known as the Common Data Set (CDS) in this book. Just enter the name of the college you are curious about and "Common Data Set" into your go-to search engine, and you are golden. The CDS is a goldmine for investigating statistics like the percentage of students who graduate in 4 or 6 years at a particular institution. A low completion rate? That is a red flag for campus vibes.

Then there is this part in the CDS where schools determine what they are looking for in applicants. For instance, some colleges like it when you show them a lot of love to prove you are keen — this could make or break your acceptance or score you a sweet financial aid. Other places might shrug off community service but give weightage to work experience. That is the kind of intel you will want when crafting your essays.

And get this: the CDS discloses information on the number of students snagged through early action or decision. But a heads-up on early decision — it is a no-go if you want to play the field with financial offers since you are locked in before other colleges show their hands. Plus, the acceptance rates for ED and EA often look more generous because that pool is stacked with top-drawer recruits, first-gen students, those needing full financial rides, and those who can pay the total price.

You will also stumble upon the dollar details — what it costs to go there, how many folks get need-based aid, and the size of the average award. Want to know how hot your potential major is? Check out how many degrees get doled out in each field.

So, that is the summary of the CDS. Now, let us turn our attention to what ChatGPT has up its sleeve about unpacking the CDS.

Prompt: You are a college admissions counselor with 20 years of experience. Your task is to reveal the common data set's benefit to a prospective college student by emphasizing important sections. Write bullet points.

ChatGPT:

Certainly! Here are some bullet points highlighting the benefits of the Common Data Set (CDS) and emphasizing its important sections for a prospective college student:

- Overview: The CDS provides standardized information about colleges and universities, making it easier for you to compare different institutions.

- Admission Statistics:

  » Get a sense of the competition by looking at the number of applicants, admitted students, and enrollment rates.

  » Check out the percentage of students accepted from the waitlist, which can give you an idea of backup plan probabilities.

- Freshman Profile:

  » View the range of SAT/ACT scores, GPAs, and class ranks of admitted students. This can help you gauge where you stand.

- Retention and Graduation Rates:

  » Understand how many students continue their education after the first year and how many graduate within 4 to 6 years, indicating student satisfaction and school effectiveness.

- Academic Offerings and Policies:

  » Gain insight into the available academic programs, popular majors, and unique opportunities at the institution.

  » Learn about special study options like study abroad or cooperative education.

- Class Size Distribution:
  - » Gauge the average class size, which can affect the quality of your educational experience, personal attention, and engagement with professors.
- Student Life:
  - » Understand the composition of the student body, including demographic details, to get a sense of the campus community.
  - » Learn about student organizations, housing, and other extracurriculars.
- Costs and Financial Aid:
  - » Get a clear picture of tuition, fees, room, and board, helping you budget and plan financially.
  - » Understand the percentage of students receiving financial aid and the average aid package size.
- Faculty:
  - » Check out faculty credentials, full-time vs. part-time faculty ratio, and the student-to-faculty ratio, indicating the potential quality of instruction.
- Campus Safety:
  - » Gain insight into campus safety, including crime statistics, which is crucial for ensuring your wellbeing.
- Transfer, Graduation, and Advanced Course Info:
  - » If you are considering transferring, you can find details about transfer admissions and policies.

» Information on advanced placement (AP) or international baccalaureate (IB) credits accepted can also be useful.

- Accreditation and Licensing:
  » Ensure the institution is accredited by recognized agencies, indicating that it meets certain standards of quality.

Using the CDS as a tool, you can make more informed decisions about which colleges or universities align with your academic and personal goals, ensuring a successful college experience.

In another prompt, I asked ChatGPT to specify how the student can leverage section B. Guess what? It produced a wrong answer. Shockingly, the same thing happened when I asked about section C21. Experimenting further, I wanted to force a correct answer. I double-checked the actual CDS and rephrased my question in the spirit of iterating. Below is my finding:

Prompt: Unfortunately, you are wrong. C21 talks about "Early Decision"... your thoughts?

ChatGPT:

You are correct, and I apologize for the confusion. Subsection C21 of the Common Data Set (CDS) indeed pertains to Early Decision (ED) policies. Understanding this section is crucial for prospective students considering an early commitment to a college or university. Here's why C21 is important:

Importance of Subsection C21: Early Decision

Understanding Early Decision Policies:

- Binding Commitment: Early Decision is a binding agreement, meaning if you are accepted, you are committed to attending that institution. C21 helps you understand the specific terms of this commitment.

- Application Deadlines: This section provides critical dates for ED applications, which are typically earlier than regular decision deadlines.

Strategic Application Planning:

- Admissions Advantage: Some colleges have higher acceptance rates for ED applicants. C21 can help you assess if applying ED might increase your chances of acceptance.

- Financial Consideration: Since ED commitments are binding, it is important to consider if you are comfortable committing before receiving financial aid packages.

Understanding ED Acceptance Rates:

- Competitiveness Insight: C21 can provide data on the number of ED applicants versus the number accepted, offering insight into the competitiveness of the ED pool.

- Yield Rate Impact: Colleges may favor ED applicants as it provides a predictable yield rate, a factor in college rankings and planning.

Plan B Strategy:

- Early Decision II Options: Some schools offer an ED II option with a later deadline, which can be a secondary strategy if the first ED choice does not pan out.
- Regular Decision Backup: Understanding ED policies helps in planning for regular decision applications if the ED application is unsuccessful.

Application Readiness:

- Early Preparation: Knowing the ED deadlines can spur early completion of college essays, recommendation letters, and standardized tests.
- Demonstrating Serious Interest: Applying ED is a strong indicator of your interest in a college, which can be a favorable factor in admissions decisions.

Impact on Senior Year:

- Early Resolution: An ED acceptance can reduce stress and uncertainty, allowing you to enjoy your senior year with a clear plan for your future.
- Continued Performance: Be aware that colleges expect you to maintain your academic performance even after an ED acceptance.

In summary, subsection C21 of the CDS is vital for understanding the nuances of Early Decision policies. It helps students make informed decisions about whether to pursue an ED application, balancing the potential advantages of a higher acceptance probability against the implications of a binding commitment and financial considerations.

The point of this chapter is to encourage the usage of ChatGPT or a similar tool for your college admissions research. The key is to remember that every answer may or may only be correct if you double-check other resources and eventually force the tool to give you the appropriate answer. Do not get me wrong, I love ChatGPT as it is a handy tool in my arsenal.

You will realize that many sections of the CDS are noteworthy for your research. The CDS is indeed a winner if appropriately used to gain insight into what the college is looking for in a prospective student on their campus. Hence, I recommend downloading the CDS from the college website and placing it under a microscope.

SCRATCH PAPER

SCRATCH PAPER

CHAPTER 13:
What I have been reading

I HAVE INCLUDED DIFFERENT VIEWPOINTS in this book to understand what people are talking about and what they care about the most. These comments are presented concisely for the larger good of the student and the parent community who can benefit from them. However, it is important to note that the following remarks are not my own and have no direct connection to my opinion on these topics. Throughout this book, my opinion may or may not match what people say. Regardless, it is crucial to respect diverse opinions and learn from them.

- Khan Academy has published extraordinary material for helping students during college admissions, including guidance on using GenAI.

- Google will hit you with endless "college essay prompts" – the truth is, nobody scrolls past page one. What counts? Write like you, a genuine teen with dreams, goof-ups, and stuff you care about. Sound magical, be bold, and let your true self shine through with all its quirks and passions.

- Dive into the Atlantic, Vanity Fair, or Rolling Stone and devour their profile pieces – that is where the magic happens. Notice how they spin stories about anything from political dramas to designer jewels yet always leave you with a vivid, clear image of the person behind the tale. That is the power of 'show, not tell' at its finest, where the essence of someone shines through in the storytelling.

- Here is a game-changer: do not just write one college essay; churn out ten, each on a wildly different slice of life. Think of your pet's untimely end, your grandma's WWII letters, or that day in algebra class when your shirt landed you in hot water. Stash them away for a week, then binge-read them all. You will spot themes peeking out, the real gold you have been digging for – raw, honest snippets that paint a picture of who you are and who you are striving to be. Grab those themes, especially the ones that feel the most real and defining and hold them tight.

- Remember that your essay is not a highlight reel of what you have done. It is a window into who you are. Make sure it is the real deal, showing a deep dive into your experiences and the lessons they have etched into you. Let it spill the beans on why you are fired up about your goals.

- The dud essays? Those who try too hard to wow the reader but end up feeling fake. Students often fall into the trap of painting their lives as super tough or one-of-a-kind, even when they are pretty run-of-the-mill.

- Choosing the right prompt can be critical for the story you are itching to tell the admissions folks. It is a no-brainer, yet you would be amazed how often it is overlooked. Do you have a killer project that aligns with your dream major or future career path? Dive deep into that, making it the star of your essay. Match it with a prompt that shines a spotlight on the best bits of what you bring to the table.

- The real deal? Most colleges will do it right for you, so trust your instinct.

- You cannot knock someone on for wanting to stay close to home or head for the hills. Campus culture and locale are legitimate game-changers because these will be your stomping grounds for a solid chunk of your life.

- No one is hitting up Harvard just for the smarts; it is the Rolodex and doors it opens, especially if Wall Street's calling your name.

- Forget about finding that one dream college. If your kid's a high school superstar, they will carve out a killer college chapter wherever they land.

- "The Daily" has the lowdown on this stuff in their podcast "The College Pricing Game – 2022/09/14". Worth a listen.

- If admissions officers raise an eyebrow at your story, expect to ride the waitlist wave.

- The onus falls on parents to manage expectations and decisions, discouraging choices driven by emotion that may lead to excessive debt and compromised educational quality.

- Choosing a college is mega, but it is wild that the decision is made in less than the time it takes to microwave popcorn by folks (college admissions officers) who are not exactly raking it in.

- The Trump offsprings are Penn proud, and with a cool $1.4 mil from Dad, they have power as alumni. It is not just about smarts – it is the network that counts.

- Sometimes, colleges look to fill a seat or balance the budget. Even if you are an AP hero with all the trimmings, there is no guarantee. And yes, that can be a tough pill to swallow after years of grinding.

- Regarding college apps, it is best to keep your cool. Stay open, do not get too hung up on any one school, and take advantage of the high school fun.

- It is all about crafting that eclectic incoming class vibe, not just rounding out every student.

- Decoding the admissions game is like trying to read tea leaves, and it is all gut and guesswork.

- Many students are rocking top-notch grades and killer ACT/SAT scores while standing out in that crowd—tough gig. Sometimes, snagging a spot at your dream school is a roll of the dice.

- If you happen to rock the exact skill a school's dying for, like ruling the waves as a coxswain or reeding it up as an oboist, you are in, assuming you tick the other boxes.

- Sports like fencing, volleyball, lacrosse for boys and lacrosse, fencing, and rifle for girls stand out, with athletics offering a potent edge in admissions.

- The unequivocal preferential treatment of athletes in college admissions is a fact.

- Harvard legacies have it sweet with a 43% acceptance rate, and those who can foot their bill get an extra look when the money talk comes around.

- Legacy might give you an edge in the Ivies, but it's no magic key to the kingdom.

- Look north, and you will find Canadian elite schools welcoming up to 35% of their students from overseas. Can't break into Stanford? McGill might roll out the red carpet, save you a bundle on tuition, and set you up sweetly for graduate school.

- Too many families get it twisted, thinking those slick college brochures in the mail are golden tickets. They are more like invites to a party you're not welcome at, especially if your statistics are mediocre.

- The school you graduate from weighs more heavily than two decades ago, a trend towards meritocracy that can significantly shape your future.

- College application pressure comes from the hometown crowd. I am dead set on pushing back while keeping it chill, being the cheerleader and the soft landing for my kids.

- Schools whip up their secret sauce when recalculating your GPA, with some giving your first-year follies a pass.

- Fluctuating academic performances and those rollercoaster grades tend to raise red flags.

- For the number crunchers out there, college rankings by big names like US News and World Reports are the go-to, but let us face it – they have also sparked some weird motivations in the race to the top. These rankings should be a foundation for further research based on individual circumstances. Students and Parents should create a ranked list per their requirements and criteria.

- Killing it in the grades department at your average high school should mean nailing those SATs or ACTs. If not, something is up.

- College often hits the wallet harder than anything else, barring a house, and yet we are throwing cash at it with barely a clue in hand.

- Get the price tag on that college dream before diving into applications. Falling head over heels for a school and then getting smacked with the reality that it is a financial no-go? That's a heartbreaker. Let's be honest: the whole college app circus is already a stress fest.

- The sticker price and how often you click on the college's website might swing things more than you would think. Embracing the unpredictable ride and switching up your top college picks is part of the game.

SCRATCH PAPER